Almost an Athlete
The Incredible Achievements of a British Transplant Runner

To Andrew,

Best Wishes

Peter Myers

Almost an Athlete

The Incredible Achievements of a British Transplant Runner

Peter Frazier

ACKNOWLEDGEMENTS

My thanks go to my wife Gill, for her encouragement, and to all my family. Special thanks to my step-daughter, Nicola, for introducing grammar, to my written text.

PREFACE

This book is the story of my life, a bit of a rollercoaster ride but I am pleased to say, with many more highs than lows. The emphasis is on certain main aspects which range between health and sport. One was the onset and effect of kidney disease when as a twenty year old, I was enjoining life as a Police Constable in Birmingham, for all intense and purposes being fit and healthy.

It then follows on to my life on dialysis, and eventual a successful kidney transplant. Then moving on to an active sporting life post transplantation, and a full life in general. The timing of my involvement in all these main aspects, purely coincidentally and unwittingly, seem to be when they were in their infancy and therefore hopefully provide some insight into their early days. This would apply to dialysis, and how this operated and was viewed by the medical profession, in the seventies. Also kidney transplantation, itself, was only in its infancy, in this country, in this decade. The first Transplant Games, was held in this country, in 1978. I competed in 1979, and was part of the management committee, for the Transplant Olympic Association, when it was formed. The emergence of the mass marathons in the UK, happened at the start of the eighties, again I ran my first Marathon, in 1981. When I look at the progression of my life, timing has been very important.

There are many reasons why I have written this book, but if it encourages one person to discuss with their family, what their wish would be if something should happen to them, which meant that organ donation was on the agenda, then I am happy. If more than one person, has the same discussion, then I am even happier.

First published 2015 by DB Publishing, an imprint of JMD Media Ltd, Nottingham, United Kingdom.

ISBN 978-1-78091-478-7

Printed and bound by Copytech (UK) Ltd, Peterborough

CONTENTS

CHAPTER 1

Something Was Wrong

It was 1970, around lunchtime, on a warm summer day, in a road located in the Handsworth district of Birmingham. As a young Police Constable, I had spent the early part of my 6am to 2pm shift covering for a lollipop lady, who for some reason had not been able to carry out her duties that morning. Standing in for Lollipop ladies was not my favourite part of the Policeman's role, I was always afraid that one of the school kids would run out into the road, under my arm, and get hit by a car. This had happened to one of my colleagues, when he was standing in for a Lollipop person. Fortunately the little girl, who did this, had not been seriously injured.

I started to feel a little faint, and after a local resident enquired if I was ok, I did admit I was feeling a little unwell. She promptly invited me into her home, to sit down, and contacted my Police Station, Thornhill Road, and advised them of my condition. They arranged for me to be collected, and returned to single men's quarters, at Holyhead Road Police Station, in Handsworth. After a couple of hours rest, I felt fine, and was able to resume my duties the next day.

I was 20 and had been a Police Officer for just over 12 months, and was very much enjoying my career in Birmingham City Police, which it was in those day prior to evolving into the West Midlands force. Being born in Birmingham, and always intending to join the Police Force at 19, I was very happy with my situation at that time, lollipop person stand-in permitting. Around this time I started to notice that my ankles had some swelling around them, so much so that my police boots were difficult to get on. I put it down to the hot summer weather, but after a few weeks decided that I had better visit my GP to have it checked out. My parents and sister lived in Yardley, on the south side of the City, and I would return home every seven days, in line with my shifts. My GP, Doctor Ince, who became a reassuring figure in my life, at that time advised there could be a number of reasons for the swelling around my ankles. After an initial blood test, carried out at the surgery and advised, "It's your kidneys".

He arranged for me to visit my local hospital, then named East Birmingham Hospital, for more in-depth blood tests. He told me I should not return to work until the extent of my condition had been understood. A further appointment, with Doctor Ince, was arranged for a few days later, when the results of my hospital tests would be available.

I felt very concerned, as I had never had much in the way of illness up to that time, apart from when as a young child, I had several bouts of tonsillitis. In the fifties, which is not the case today, most young sufferers had their tonsils removed. At the age of six, mine were removed, and to demonstrate how times have changed, in terms of lengths of stay in hospital, I remember asking a nurse, on my third day in hospital, if I was going home that day, and she replied, "You haven't had your tonsils out yet". I was also concerned about my police career, when reporting sick and was not specific about the problem I had.

On my return to see my Doctor, he told me that the test results had come back from East Birmingham Hospital, and they had confirmed there was a problem, with my kidneys. He said that my condition was called Nephritis, which was basically inflammation of the kidneys. They were enlarged, and the job that they were doing was adversely affected. Over the next few years I was to understand more of the workings of the kidneys. He said that I would need to see a consultant at the hospital. He would write to them and they would send me an appointment.

After a few days, an appointment arrived, and I was off to see John Hawkins,

Renal Consultant, at East Birmingham Hospital. Doctor Hawkins was a doctor who cared very much about his patients, and I always felt that I could not have had better medical support at that time. He was a real character, drove a Morgan car, wore a Russian hat, was a Navigation Officer in the Naval Reserve, and without any doubt, was and is a top man.

During my first consultations with Doctor Hawkins, he informed me that various drugs had been tried for the condition I had and it could be a case of trying one or two of these. I don't recall enquiring as to what happened if they didn't work, and don't recall that he offered the information either. I think this may have been deliberate on his part, but it maybe that if I had asked the question he would have answered honestly, which is probably why I did not ask the question, in dread of what the answer might be. I did enquire what had caused me to have Nephritis, after being generally healthy throughout my life up to that time and he advised that it was probably caused by a virus that had attacked my kidneys. My blood pressure was higher than it should be, and beta-blockers were prescribed. I often wonder if my tonsils had not been removed, whether they may have taken the brunt of this virus, and my kidneys may not have been affected. I don't know the answer to this question, and I am not sure a medical man would know either. The swelling of my ankles and legs was caused by fluid build-up and I recall being given some (diuretic) tablets, which over the course of a couple days reduced my weight from about 12 stone to my normal 10 stone.

I am about 5' 8" tall, which was a minimum height requirement in those days, to join most Police Forces apart from the Metropolitan Force, known as the 'Met' covering London. There the minimum height was 5'10". When I went for my initial interviews, I was the only prospective recruit who was measured by the Inspector rather than the sergeant who had measured all the others. After getting me to stand up straight, against the wooden measure, the Inspector uttered "5' 8"", which was duly noted. My actual height I believe was closer to 5' 7" and a half inches, and I am sure that the fact I had an Uncle, who was a senior officer, in Birmingham City Police at that time, had nothing to do with this slight exaggeration of my height. In my early days in the force, I was assigned to various Resident Beat Officers, who were officers responsible for a particular area of the patch. Young officers were rotated to join these experienced officers for a few days to get to know the area. One of the Resident Beat Officers was about 6'7" tall, and when I was walking along side of him we must have looked quite comical, which brought the comment of some school children, when we passed a playground of, "It's Mr little Policeman."

I had not returned to work, as instructed, by my GP, but had been submitting Doctors Notes, to the station, covering my absence. After about four months, I received a letter which requesting my permission for the Police Surgeon (Police Medical Advisor) to write to my Consultant, regarding my condition, which I duly gave. I did not give this much thought, just assumed it was a routine procedure in cases like mine. A couple of weeks later I received a letter asking me to attend a meeting, at Tally Ho, the local Police Headquarters, with the Police Surgeon. The meeting, although handled very sympathetically, basically was to inform me that my police career was at an end. The response he had received from Dr Hawkins, my Consultant, stated that I would only be able to carry out desk duties, and probably went into more details about my longer term prognosis, which obviously was not good. The first two years in the Police Force is probationary, and for whatever reason if a recruit is unable to carry out their duties to the full, then, as in my case, they do not make the position into the permanent status.

I was devastated as the Police force was the only career that I ever wanted to do. The force did try to help in finding me a civilian role, and I did visit the Finger Print department to look at a possible role there. This, together with other possible police civilian placements turned out to be fruitless, due to the fact Superannuation (Pension) was applicable to these jobs, and a medical examination was mandatory, which at that point, I was not going to pass. Jobs were much easier to find in those days and within two weeks of leaving the

Police Force, I was in employment, as a Progress Clerk (a desk based role), in the Purchasing Office, at Serck Radiators, located in Greet, Birmingham B11.

Our house, in Yardley, was small. My bedroom was basically a box room, and we had no central heating. We decided to look for a more suitable house, and we found it in Denise drive, Kingshurst. I had a much larger bedroom, and the previous occupant, was a central heating engineer. As well as the various drug treatments, that I was given, I was also subject to a very restrictive diet routine, which was almost impossible to totally adhere to. About 600 mls of fluid intake maximum (equivalent of about two and half cups of tea a day), high protein food, and the most difficult; low salt. Basically everything has salt in it, to some extent; bread, cereals, anything tinned, or processed products. One of the main things that I found difficult to cope with, was not being able to have gravy, which to this day gives me bad memories of trying to eat dry food at my grandmothers, who I visited once a week, she was just following instructions, no salt, and no gravy.

Again in the 1970's, specific foods such as low salt, gluten free, etc. were almost not existent, whereas today food products for most medical and other needs are widely available. Also, as a result of my condition, my taste buds changed, and I could not eat certain foods; fish, I remember, became a problem to eat. Sugar was not a problem, virtually without restriction. One of the main areas of concern for people with renal failure is the build-up of potassium. Kidneys which are functioning normally will ensure that the potassium in the body is kept at the required level. A high amount of potassium in the body can stop your heart, which does not take a medical person to understand is pretty much terminal. Potassium is high in root vegetables, and therefore kidney patients are told to boil vegetables that come under this category. It can be seen that the diet regime, for a person with some level of renal failure, was quite difficult for the patient, and also the immediate family to cope with. The good news was I could eat as many boiled sweets as I wanted.

Whether I was naive or did not wish to think about it, I basically thought my health situation would stay the same or would improve. I had viewed some television documentary, around this time showing people who were having dialysis. It looked horrific to me, like being in an iron lung for hours and hours, but obviously, to my mind, my condition was nothing as serious as that, and was virtually blanked from my mind.

There were certain procedures and tests that were carried out over the next few months. Some of which involved a day or so in hospital, other were just a couple of hours. These included a biopsy, where a piece of kidney was taken, and various X-rays. Some of these X-rays would include the introduction of a dye into the blood. X-rays would be taken every few minutes to provide the medical staff with the flow of the dye, around my body, and detail of my renal function. I was having regular check-ups at the hospital, where they would take blood and urine, and usually give me the results at my next appointment. It was coming up to about two years after my initial diagnosis. I had had a heavy cold and been for my hospital appointment and had the usual tests. A couple of days after my check up, I received a letter from the hospital, 'could I make an urgent appointment to see Dr Hawkins?' which I did. When I saw Doctor Hawkins, he said that my blood results had shown a deterioration, and I was now at a point where I needed to have dialysis. This was a total shock to me, as dialysis had never been mentioned before, and the thought of having to go on a kidney machine was disturbing. The rest of what he was saying to me was a bit of a blur. He was saying that I would need to have an operation on my arm, to provide a fistula. This is basically the joining the vein, in my arm, to an artery, to allow the needles to be inserted, part of dialysis process. He said another blood test would be carried out to confirm the latest results.

I had recently had a heavy cold, just prior to the tests and next blood results were not as bad as the originals, however, it was till decided that I should go on dialysis without much delay, as it was close to where without it, I would not survive. It would give the hospital a few extra weeks for the operation to create a fistula, to take place, and the commencement of the dialysis could be arranged.

At this time around the middle of 1972, in the UK, dialysis, was not available for anyone under 15, or over 55. This was a combination of expense and also medical thinking at that time, in terms of coping with the process, and the prognosis, for that demographic. Although dialysis had been around for a few years, it was a much more involved procedure, than with the current equipment used. There was a variance in views in the medical world, in terms of dialysis and transplantation, as I will go into later in this book. East Birmingham Hospital had a Renal Unit, with the main activity being to train people who required dialysis to have their dialysis at home. This usually took about three months, during which time their dialysis was carried out in the Unit. Three months was basically a minimum period, however some patients took a lot longer, and some, I think remained a permanent fixture in the unit.

Even if you were between the ages of 15 and 55, it was not automatic that you would be accepted to go on the dialysis programme. The Hospital had to be sure the patient had the support and backup at home, to cope with home dialysis. In my case, I was living with my parents, and I also had an older sister, Sandra, at home. I think I was also regarded as a stable individual, who would do as instructed, and would hopefully be able to cope. I was accepted on the programme and arrangements were made for the fistula operation and a date to commence dialysis at the unit.

My fistula operation was carried out under a local anaesthetic. I remember, whilst on the operating table, being asked by the nurse tasked with keeping an eye to me, if I wanted to have a look at the operation while it was going on?

I replied, "Not really."

However, I did look up to the large reflective operating light above, and saw what looked like an array of veins and clamps, arranged round the area of my left lower arm, and quickly looked away. I am not a squeamish person when it comes to watching operations, but that is usually on the television, with someone else on the table. The operation seems to take quite a long time, during which was asked a few times if I could feel anything, as they would increase the anaesthetic if necessary. I've since found out the some surgeons only like to do this operation under a general anaesthetic.

After the operation, back in bed, on the ward, my arm was put in a sling. The vein was basically swollen, to be used for the needle site. When you touch the vein it buzzed, which was a test to see whether it is working or not. Knowing that I was somewhat down, my dad had managed to get hold of two tickets for the FA Cup semi-final, which involved my football team, Birmingham City and the then high-riding team, Leeds United, that season. The match was at Hillsborough, Sheffield Wednesday's impressive ground. It struck me as being a little unfair that the semi-final was being played there, as Sheffield is in Yorkshire, and Leeds is a Yorkshire club, but I think this was just sour grapes on my part. I recall walking up to the ground with my arm in a sling, and aware of the buzzing sensation. Leeds United were at the height of their supremacy. At that time Leeds had a routine before games, of coming out of the tunnel and to start doing exercises, as a team, around the centre circle. In an effort to get one up on Leeds, Birmingham got out first, made their way to the centre circle and proceeded to do their own version of the Leeds warm up. This amused my fellow 'blues' supporters, but did not affect the Leeds team in any way, apart from motivating the hot favourites. They went on to win 3–0, with a typical professional performance.

My initial dialysis was booked in for six weeks after the fistula operation, which is the usual timescale it takes, for the veins to expand, strengthen, and be ready for use. I was also going to visit the Renal Unit to prepare me for the future dialysis. It turned out not to be the reassuring experience the medical staff were hoping for.

CHAPTER 2

Hospital Dialysis

The Renal Unit at East Birmingham Hospital, was a single floor, separate building, linked to the main Hospital by a corridor. The Dialysis area, itself, comprised a room for the nurses, some single rooms, mainly for new patients, and a central room with about eight beds, each with a kidney machine next to it, next to the nurses' room. The rest of Unit, on the left hand side, after going in through the main entrance, was made up of Doctor rooms, the office area, and also an area where the technicians, who looked after the Kidney Machines and equipment, both in the Unit and at patients' homes, were based. There was also an area that patients, who were close to finishing their training, could use, which replicate home dialysis conditions. Hygiene was a top priority in the Unit, anyone entering the dialysis area, was required to wash their hands and they walked in through over a disinfected pad, and also cover their shoes with elasticised plastic overshoes. Strict times were observed for visitors, and a strong regimented regime existed.

On the day I was shown round the Unit by Doctor Hawkins, with the emphasis on showing me the dialysis process for my reassurance, things did not go as well as they might. After an initial look around, Dr Hawkins enquired of the nursing staff, if anyone was about to be prepared for dialysis. "Yes, we are about to put the needles into Raglan's arm," was the reply.

I was then ushered forward to watch the process. Raglan Weir was a big, black guy, about 40 years of age, who ran a shop, in Handsworth. (His son, Bob Weir, later represented Great Britain regularly, in discus, and was a top athlete for many years). I was to see a lot of Raglan, over the next few months, and became friendly with him, as we dialysed on the same days. In hindsight, I doubt if the nursing staff felt they had made a good choice in using Raglan, for my first viewing of the dialysis process. The two needles used, one for the blood to come out of the body, and the other to re-enter the body, after being through the dialysis process, which I will describe later, are about three millimetres in diameter. A local anaesthetic is used to freeze the vein, before these needles are inserted. Raglans veins were huge, resulting from the fistula operation. Usually patients have to insert their needles themselves, but he had been having some problems, so the nursing staff had stepped in. The initial anaesthetic had been inserted into Raglan's vein, and the nursing staff were now attempting to insert the first needle.

"Oh! It's blown!" the nurse exclaimed, and pressure was immediately applied to Raglan's vein. This was something that can happen it was explained to me, generally when fistulas are recent and expanded veins have yet strengthened. They would leave it a few minutes then try again. After several more attempts the nursing staff had failed to successfully insert the needles into Raglans veins. It had been about an hour since I had been ushered forward to watch this routine process. I was told afterwards that I was looking a little pale at that point, and someone had taken the decision to drag me away. If this initial look was designed to reassure me about what I was about to experience, it certainly was failing badly.

The day had arrived for me to commence my dialysis, this was about six weeks after I had had the fistula created. In future weeks, as was the system in the Renal Unit, I would set up the dialysis equipment myself, as patients were required to do, after training. This usually took about 30 minutes. Today the equipment had been set up for me. In those days weekly dialysis was required for about 28–30 hours a week. As current dialysis equipment is much more efficient this period is reduced to about 12–14 hours a week, for an adult. At that time patients usually did two 14 hour periods, a week, and would be in the Unit overnight, but as this was my first time my dialysis was shorter, and I would be going home that evening. Doctor Hawkins was in attendance, and the process of connecting me to the equipment commenced. Anaesthetic was inserted into my arm and insertion of one of the needles began. Immediately my vein began to swell, and the needle was withdrawn, and pressure applied.

"Don't worry, this can sometimes happen with a new fistula," was the chorus of reassurance. Thankfully, after a second attempt, dialysis could commence. After removal of some clamps, I watched the blood run out of my body, through the tube from the needle, into the keel (later described) and back into my body, via the second needle. There was no sensation as such, just lying in bed, with two tubes filled with red blood, attached to your arm, knowing you were connected to the machine, and basically that is where you were remaining for the next few hours, until disconnected. Around tea time the nurse poked her head round the door of my single room, and advised that tea had arrived.

"Ah," she said, "We have told the chef about this before. I am afraid he has sent in braised kidneys for your meal! If it's a problem, I will see if we can get something else for you!"

"No, don't worry, I'll have them," I replied, with a grin on my face. I drove home, that night with a positive attitude about my situation, but not really sure why!

Whilst building up my dialysis hours, over the first few sessions, up to the usual 14 hours, I was quickly encouraged and required, by the Unit's nursing staff, to learn to set up the equipment prior to dialysis. The philosophy was all geared to get you ready to dialyse, at home, as quickly as possible, which would be your future. I also resolved to insert the needles myself, as soon as possible. My thinking being that if this is inevitable let's get on with it. I was not keen on needles, injections, blood being taken, and the like, but soon realised that they only hurt, if you don't relax. Having said that I realise there are people who hate needles, and recall one poor guy, who was in this position. He would get into a real state, when it came to having his needles inserted, prior to dialysis. This usually followed the path of screens being pulled round his bed, whilst two or three nursing staff, would carry out the process of inserting his needles, to some distressing screams from this agitated patient.

My boss at work was very obliging and allowed me two afternoons off a week, whilst I was training and dialysing, at the Renal Unit. I would work in the morning, travel to the unit after lunch set up and dialysis for 14 hours, overnight, and return to work the following morning. After a couple of weeks, I was inserting my own needles, and setting up the dialysis equipment. It was then only necessary to get one of the nursing staff to help me start the dialysis process, basically consisting of releasing clamps etc. At home this would usually be done by a family member, in my case my dad, or sister. I did not think it possible but I did come across some home dialysis patients, some years hence, who managed to carry out the process without assistance. They had my admiration, I don't think I would have attempted this myself, whilst totally alone.

The initial focus that is made clear to you, is that hygiene is essential. Needles are being inserted and blood is going out of the body and coming back. Basic nursing procedures, in terms of hand washing, wearing gloves, how sterilised packs are to be opened, are therefore part of the training. Needles and lines to be used are disposed of after the process. Saline is used and run through the line prior to the blood be circulated. The dialysis equipment then consisted the machine itself, which was a free standing rectangular unit, on casters. About four feet high, and around three foot square, with the two large dials on the front. Alarms would sound, and would need to be reset, if flow or temperature, went outside the set tolerances. The machine itself would provide the fluid, containing electrolytes which the body needs, but are lost when the body is in renal failure. This fluid would flow though the other part of the dialysis equipment, called a keel, which was basically the artificial kidney. This was made up of three polypropylene plates, about three foot long, eighteen inches wide, and an inch think. Between these plates, would be two sets of membranes, of a clear cellophane material, which is where the blood, would go through. By a process of osmosis the impurities in the blood were taken out, whilst the electrolytes, were transferred into the blood returning to the body.

Without delay, the patient was required to carry out all the work necessary to be able to carry out dialysis in their home. This included, at the end of the dialysis, the dismantling of the keel, washing, sterilising, and reassembling, ready for the next use. The keel was bolted together and needed to be dismantled, and reassembled, by way of a ratchet spanner. Once dismantled the three boards were placed in a bath and thoroughly washed, and a formalin solution was used to ensure no blood remained. Formalin is formaldehyde, diluted in water, which gives out a pungent gas, it therefore needed to be handled with care, as any laboratory operative, will confirm. The reassembling, ready for dialysis required the two sets of cellophane to be placed in between the polypropylene boards, and the whole keel bolted together, using the ratchet spanner. Once assembled the keel would be tested to ensure that there were no holes in the membranes, allowing blood leaks. This was done by means of the use of a pressure gauge. If the pressure through the membranes outside of the specified tolerance, it meant that the keel had failed, and the keel had to be rebuilt, which was basically starting from scratch. On many occasions, after dialysing for 14 hours, I found my blood pressure was quite low, and carrying out the process of dismantled, washing, building the keel etc., was hard to do. The Unit staff however, had instructions not to help, and unless the patient was really unable, they would insist it was done. The whole emphasis, as previously stated, was to replicate what would happen at home, and therefore, this is how they were required to operate.

It was the summer of 1972, and the world's greatest sporting event, was about to happen, the Olympics were imminent and I got hold of a small television, to be placed by my bed in the Renal Unit, so I could ensure I did not miss the action, whilst dialysing. The 1972 Olympics were held in Munich. It will be remembered for the things that happened in the Games Village. The hostage situation, threatened the whole event, that year, but fortunately the event went ahead, after the distressing incident. Global events such as the Olympics, may always be a target for terrorist actions, the organisers, with the help of the international community, can only being vigilant and do everything to ensure that terrorists do not succeed. I had always been a great fan of athletics, especially middle distance running, although I had no personal background of any other running, apart from being able to hold my own in a sprint at school sports. I recall watching great performances, on the track.

One that comes to mind, happened in the 1964 Tokyo Olympics when a British lady named Ann Packer, who was one of the favourites to win her main event the 400 metres. She did not take the gold medal in the 400 metres, but did manage to come second and win the silver medal. She was also entered in the 800 metres, although this was not an event she was recognised as a main contender for. In the final Ann was behind quite a few runners, on the final bend coming into the straight, suddenly she appeared from nowhere, and using her 400 metre runner pace, overtook everyone and kept going to the finishing line to win the gold. One of the great British Olympic performances of all time. At the finish she spotted her future husband, Robbie Brightwell, and ran over to him. Robbie himself was a top 400 metre runner, who provided some great sporting moments usually when he was part of the 400 metre relay team. He later won silver in the 4 x 400 metres relay, in Tokyo, an event with a great tradition of Great Britain performing well.

I always thought how great it would be to represent Great Britain, and win a medal for your country.   So for the next three months, my life revolved around two lots of 14 hours of dialysis a week, at the unit. Trying to cope with a very restricted diet, and generally surviving within the confined existence. The message from the Renal Unit was 'Dialyse to Live, not live to dialyse', in practise you needed to get on with it. Your prospects were to survive through 'home dialysis', this was your long term future. When transplantation was mentioned, at East Birmingham Hospital, it was in terms of, 'a short term break from dialysis', 'they don't work in the long term, maybe a few months, a year or so before they fail'. There was a transplant list, which the hospital did not consider placing you on, until your home dialysis had settled down, and you were coping well with it. The timescale was usually about 12 months after you had started home dialysis. You were asked if you wanted to be on the transplant list, initially, and then if you did, you were written to regularly, to ask if you wanted to stay on the list. This was all against the background that the medical staff, and even some dialysis patients that you met, would give negative messages, sometime horror stories, regarding unsuccessful transplants. The problem was that you were only going to meet people who had returned to dialysis after bad experiences with transplantation, because the people who had had transplants, which had worked in the longer term, you would not come across in the Unit.

In total contrast to this, the Queen Elizabeth Hospital, in Birmingham, which was then carrying out kidney transplant operations, had a totally different philosophy. They had a dialysis unit, where patients' dialysed as a stopgap until they were able to get a kidney for them. The operation was totally geared to get them a transplant, when a suitable kidney could be found. The programme there had been started in the early 1970s, under the guidance, of Consultant Surgeon, Tony Barnes. He was a highly respected figure, who would be seen, around the QE Hospital, wearing a dickey bow, usually with a smile on his face, and offering a humorous remark. He was once given the title of 'Midlander of the Year', and was, without doubt one of the major people to advance transplantation, in the Midlands, at that time. I would, through various involvements later in my life, come in contact with Tony Barnes regularly, and hold him in high regard.

My training at the Renal Unit had progressed well and, in line with the minimum time of three months, I was pretty much ready to transfer my dialysis to the home environment. My bedroom at home had been converted into a room suitable for dialysis to take place. Plumbing work had been carried out, including the installation of a sink, and taps. Shelves had been fitted, necessary for the various dialysis supplies, such as sterile packs, lines saline etc. Plus, equipment such has clamps, pressure gauge, and ratchet spanner, had been delivered. There can be various spillages, with the dialysis process, so the other main provision in my bedroom, was a heavy duty linoleum, on the floor, which continued a few inches up the walls, and was thoroughly sealed, to avoid any leaks. Once the bedroom was ready the kidney machine and keel was delivered. It was fortunate that my bedroom was a big enough to cope with all the equipment, plus my bed and leave room to move around. Some patients who did not have this amount of room, had their houses altered, by the local authority, and even extensions were built.

The only thing left to happen before I could go home was for me to go into the home training room, at the unit, for two weeks, where one of my helpers would assist me, as would happen at home. It was decided, dad would do this, although at home this assistance would be shared by my sister and him. Dad would assist me in the evening, to go on, and then in the morning, before he went to work, he would drive to the Unit, and assist me to disconnect again. This all went reasonably smoothly, so I was given my discharge papers, and Unit dialysis was behind me in favour of home dialysis.

CHAPTER 3

Home Dialysis

Instead of the two fourteen hour sessions, as was my dialysis at the unit, my home dialysis would be three ten hour sessions; Monday, Wednesday, and Friday. My sister, Sandra, would assist me in the evening, and my dad would assist me in the morning. Generally I would go upstairs and be dialysing from about 8.30pm, (problems with my veins, getting needles in, and the keel pressure permitting). In the morning, I would be disconnected about 6.30am. Then the keel had to be dismantled, washed, sterilised, and rebuilt as previously described. I would then be off to work, sometimes not feeling terribly good if my blood pressure was on the low side. If all went well, then at least there was some respite from dialysis, on Tuesday, Thursday, and weekends. However if there was a problem on Monday night, for example I could not get my needles in and I had to dialyse on Tuesday, the whole of the week was disrupted. The whole of family existence now revolved around dialysis.

In 1973, I changed my job. I was appointed to the post of Assistant Buyer, at Alcan Plate Ltd, in Kitts Green, Birmingham. Whilst working at Serck, in the Buying Office as a Progress Clerk, I had come to the conclusion that 'Purchasing/Buying', might be a good career to get into, so I looked around and found this position, which also was a little closer to my home. I was surprised that I was given the job bearing in mind my health situation, which I had fully advised them of. I was appreciative of the consideration, that the management of

Serck had shown me, in terms of time off and their general assistance, but I felt they thought of me, with my health problems, as just someone who would stay in that basic position. I knew to find a job to put me on a career path I would have to move on. It was a coincidence, that my cousin David Frazier, who was an Engineer, joined Serck, a week after I left. Someone in the company, who was obviously unaware that I had left, rang him up, a few days later, only checking the surname, from the internal directory, thinking I was him.

I was generally fortunate, in terms of my health, as most of the time I felt reasonably well. Although, I gradually acquired a pale complexion, and looking back over my passport photo at that time, was quite gaunt looking. Due to the restrictive diet, my weight did decline over a period of time, but this was a very gradually process. Social life was restricted, and holidays, without dialysis, were just a three or four day break. The hospital did have a holiday caravan, in the grounds of a small hospital, based in Weymouth. The caravan had dialysis facilities there and you were able to book a few days down there, if you could get in early enough. We as a family did use this facility during two or three summers. It was necessary to take supplies down there and it was made clear that, although in the grounds of the hospital, on no account should the patient bother the hospital, as they were nothing to do with the facility. I recall that I did bother them once, as we had a broken clamp, and they could not be more obliging.

On one of our holidays in the dialysis caravan in Weymouth, we took the opportunity, to travel to Guernsey in the Channel Islands, via the Weymouth ferry. My Aunt and Uncle, Joan and Roy, were on holiday there and we managed to book accommodation for a couple of days. Straight after dialysis, we got on the ferry around lunchtime, and in hindsight made the wrong decision, in terms of lunch. For some reason, I decided on a Ploughman's lunch. I think this was one of my rebellious days, stretching my diet to the limit. As soon as the ferry starting moving into the channel, I regretted my decision; I started and continued to be seasick for the next four hours, until we arrived at St Peter Port, in Guernsey.

Meeting up with our relatives, at the port, we had a very pleasant time looking round the island, which we had not previously visited. I had never been a heavy smoker, and I did pack up completely in my mid- twenties, but I did smoke at that time. Cigarettes were ridiculously cheap in the Channel Islands, so I took the opportunity to try a few different brands, including menthol ones such as St Moritz! One evening we decided to play cards, back at my Aunt and Uncle's digs. It was decided to take something to drink back to their room. Knowing that I was restricted to what I could drink, they asked me what I liked to drink. I replied Vodka, which was my usual tipple at that time, although I was never a heavy drinker.

"How about Bloody Mary?" (Vodka and Tomato Juice), it was suggested.

I do not particularly like tomato juice, but as this was agreed generally I was willing to go along with the joint decision. Every time I took a drink of the Bloody Mary, whilst playing cards, I would make the sound of "Urrgh!" pulled my tongue out and winced, but I carried on drinking it.

Around this time, along with my sister, I got involved with the East Birmingham Hospital Kidney Patients Association. Many of the dialysis hospitals up and down the country had these associations, and also a national federation was established. Basically, the KPAs, represented the patients, kept them updated, both with happenings at the hospital and in the wider world of dialysis. They also provided social events for them and their families, and generally concerned themselves with the patients, welfare. The East Birmingham Hospital KPA, was made up of about six or seven people. The chairman was John Ford, and the committee consisted of his wife Gill, Tom Johnson, Graham Barnes and his wife Sandra, Lesley Hewitt, myself and my sister. John, Tom, Graham, Lesley and myself, were all home dialysis patients. We had various ways of raising funds for the KPA, in order that we could carry out our activities. In the summer we would participate in many of the local fetes, with a variety of things on our stall to encourage the visiting public to spend. This would include Tombola, hitting the rat in the drainpipe, selling sweets and pop, etc. Many a Saturday afternoon, would see us at the local summer fete, with the abiding memory of John shouting, "Fizzy pop ten pence," from our stall. These summer activities basically became our social life, and without doubt the general camaraderie and fun, helped make, what was a difficult existence, bearable.

We would have an EBHKPA Christmas party, were the kids of the patients would all be given a Christmas present. At one Christmas party, a relative of one of the committee had volunteered to be our Father Christmas. The outfit had been acquired, all it needed was for this elderly man to come in to the main hall of the school that we had hired in his red outfit, say a few Ho! Ho! Ho's, and give out the presents, when the kids were called up.

I thought we had reached this point, so I got onto the stage, and exclaimed, in the usual build up way, "OK, kids, I understand a special visitor has just arrived. He has a white beard, and a red coat, do you know who it is?"

"Father Christmas!" was the unanimous response. "OK, well if you all sit down and keep quiet, he will come in and have some presents for you," I advised.

At which point I looked for his entrance from the side door. Nothing happened, so I advised the audience he would be in any second. A few seconds more, still no sign. Then things started to come into my head, like he has had a problem parking the sleigh, he just had to feed Rudolf. These things kept coming into my head, and all I could do was keep telling the kids, that this or that had caused the delay. I was getting the odd person appear at the side door and prompting me to keep going. Eventually, after what seemed like about 20 minutes, the figure of Father Christmas appeared, and I heaved a sigh of relief. I never did get a full explanation of why he was so delayed, just some garbled statement of having trouble getting the outfit on was as much as I was told.

We decided to put on a pantomime, for one of the Christmas parties. Not sure how I got the job of writing this dubious piece of storytelling, but we certainly had some fun in producing it. Cinderella was the chosen pantomime, with a hospital background. The main part of Cinderella was played by Lesley; Tom and John were cast as the ugly sisters, and when we were short of people from the committee we dragged in a few friends to play some of the minor parts. I played a doctor, with just a couple of lines to say, however I wore a Russian hat, so when I appeared on stage, everyone knew who I was impersonating, including Doctor Hawkins, who was in the audience. I think there were some laughs from that direction. I have been involved in quite a few things in my life, but I can honestly say that for fun and laughs, this was the most enjoyable project, I have been concerned with. The laughs were mainly at the rehearsals, in the lounge of John's house. There was a particular line that Tom always struggled with, in his role as an ugly sister. Whilst Tom delivered his line, in full seriousness, the rest of us were rolling around with laughter, as we knew it was coming out wrong again.

We held the dress rehearsal, as with our other rehearsals, in John's lounge. For anyone who was walking past his home that evening, they must have wondered what was going on, with Lesley in her impressive ball gown, and Tom and John dressed in their ugly sister outfits. I don't think our production would have ever won a Bafta, but I think the audience appreciated our efforts in putting it on.

My other main form of enjoyment, if that is the word, was following my football team, Birmingham City. Over the years, to be a Birmingham City supporter, you need to be something of a masochist, although somewhere, in the mind of the dedicated 'Blues' supporter, there is a belief that one day they may achieve great things. Even when my team managed to win the League Cup in 2011, they immediately contrived to get themselves relegated from the Premier League at the end of the season. My sister also got the bug for Football, around this time, and we would travel to many of the away games, as well as attending the home games. The team boasted some good players in the seventies, the likes of Trevor Francis, Bob Latchford, Kenny Burns, amongst them. Jasper Carrot, probably the best known Birmingham supporter, does a routine about when Birmingham played Manchester United, at Old Trafford, which would have been about the mid-seventies. My sister and I were at this game, which he described, and although he uses a little humorous licence his description is quite close to the truth. In those days Old Trafford capacity was just over 50,000. On this day the Birmingham support consisted of about 200 dedicated followers, with a certain absence of blue scarves. We were located in one small section, on the side, of the ground, surrounded by the home support, all of whom seemed to be waving their red scarves. The first half started and Birmingham were performing quite well against the illustrious opposition. Then Kenny Burns appeared in front of goal and slotted the ball into the net, in one action the Blues supporters rose to applaud the goal, but also sat down pretty quickly, when they realised they were surrounded by 50,000 United supporters, who we not used to being behind at home, and did not appreciate the fact. As the half went on United made their presence felt and equalised. In Jasper's story, he and his mate went for some refreshment at half time. Jasper's mate, came out with the immortal line, as he got to the counter of, "Oy! Carrot, they ain't got no cowing Bovril."

The second half commenced and again Birmingham had the audacity to take the lead for a second time. Again we Blues supporters rose to celebrate the goal, but this time, we returned to our seats quicker than on the first occasion, having taken in the reaction to the first goal. United reacted and it was not long before they equalised. The game ended in a 2–2 draw and for the Blues contingent it was a moral victory. We promptly left the ground with our heads held high, and our blue scarves well hidden.

In the 2010–11 season Birmingham City finally won a major trophy, the League Cup, although they had won in the League Cup previously in the 1962–63 session when they beat City rivals Aston Villa, in a two legged Final. I don't remember much about this at the time, but it was not such a big deal as in recent years. Unfortunately, the victory in 2011, was dulled by the fact that the team were relegated from the Premiership at the end of the season.

The two legged semi-final against West Ham United had provided some concerning moments. Not least that the 'Blues' were trailing 1–0, after the first leg away, and then conceded an early goal at St Andrews. The irony was that West

Ham were now owned by David Sullivan, and the Gold Brothers, who were the previous owners of Birmingham City. At two nil down, our then Manager Alex McLeish, bought on our 6'8" tall centre forward, Nikola Zigic at the start of the second half. With the impact of Zigic, and some great finishing by Craig Gardner, a local lad and self proclaimed 'Blue Nose', the home team scraped through, with a 3–2 victory.

A great day out for the Blues fans at the 'New Wembley', was the prospect. Although as the opposition were Arsenal, who had not won a trophy for a few years, at that time there were not many people giving my team much of a chance. Over the years the meetings with Arsenal had usually ended in only one result, which was not a win for the 'Blues'. I do remember, however, when we played Arsenal in the FA Cup in 1968. The first game was at Highbury, which was Arsenal previous Ground before the Emirates. The old ground was famous for having a large clock, in the centre of one of the ends. I had travelled to the game with my dad, and a friend of ours. Birmingham conceded in the first half, and our chances of progressing in the competition that year did not look good. With two or three minutes left we had given up and were making our way towards the exit. This was long before all seater stadiums, and people tended to walk up the terraces, close to the end of a game. Birmingham were on the attack, so we turned to watch before we exited the ground. The ball was crossed to one of our forwards, Geoff Vowden, who was positioned on the edge of Arsenal's penalty area. Vowden headed the ball upwards towards the goal. The Arsenal goalkeeper jumped with hands high to claim the ball. Inexplicably the ball went straight through his hands and into the net. I don't think I have seen a headed goal like that before or after this event. A goalkeeping error, but one that the Blues supporters were not complaining about, and a replay back at St Andrews.

The replay took place on the following Wednesday. It would have been a cold night so I took a flask of tea with me in my coat pocket. I stood on the kop and as the kick off approached more and more people seem to surround me. The atmosphere that night was tremendous. I seemed to be moving round with the crowd throughout the game. The flask stayed in my pocket as I did have room to put my hand in my pocket to retrieve it. Football wise the team were excellent and were worthy 2–0 winners, and through to the next round of the Cup. The next day it was reported that several thousand people had got in to see the game without paying. There had been a hole in the fence and supporters had taken the opportunity to enter by this means. It was estimated that approaching 60,000 people attended the game that night, far exceeding the ground capacity. That year Birmingham got through to the semi-final of the FA Cup, after beating Chelsea 1–0 in the next round, at St Andrews. The FA Cup semi-final was at Villa Park, against West Bromwich Albion, who went on to win the Cup that year.

Back to the Final in 2011, I travelled to the final at Wembley, by coach, with my sister, Sandra, and my uncle Richard. We had seats in the top tear, on the side. Arsenal were four to one on favourites, but we had a team with a heart. In the third minute our veteran midfielder, Lee Bowyer, looked to be onside, only to be flagged offside, after being clattered by the young Arsenal Goalkeeper Szczesny. Most certainly a penalty, if Bowyer was onside, and pretty much an inevitable red card for the goalkeeper. The television coverage showed that Bowyer was definitely onside, but who knows whether the result would have changed had Arsenal gone down to ten men at that point.

As the game progressed Birmingham were holding their own, getting into the faces of the opposition and curtailing their passing game. Midway through the first half Birmingham took the lead from a corner. The ball came to Roger Johnson, our centre-half, who was positioned on the edge of the penalty area. Johnson, who spent much of the second half limping, but typically refused to be substituted, headed the ball forward, towards the goal. The tall Nikola Zigic who was standing close to the 'keeper, did not have to jump, but produced a deft header into to the net. Jubilation and shock from the Blues fans, stunned silence and shock from the Arsenal fans. The Blues players continued to play positively, but just before the break, Robin Van Persie, Arsenal's lethal striker pounced, to level the game.

In the second half, the game continued to be in the balance, and could have been settled, when Birmingham midfielder Fahey, hit the post, and the ball travelled across the goal. In the last fifteen to twenty minutes, Arsenal started to get on top, requiring the excellent Birmingham and England goalkeeper, Ben Foster to produce three or four good saves. Birmingham Manager, Alex McLeish sent on striker, Obafemi Martins, with a few minutes to go. In the 89th minute, the ball came through to Szczesny, he and his defender, seemed to look to each other and neither dealt with ball. Martins was on hand about four yards out to slot the ball home. I don't know whether it was the same for other Blues' fans, but to me it seemed an age before Obafemi Martins kicked the ball in the next. When I have watched it again on the TV, he did not hesitate when the ball came to his feet, but on the day, its three or four seconds. Anyway he scored, and goes down in blues folklore as scoring the goal that gave Birmingham there first major trophy since 1963. Ben Foster was given man of the match, deservedly for his second half saves, but there must be special mention for Lee Bowyer, who never stopped running, and never pulled out of a challenge, and I am sure ended the day with a few bruises.

Travelling home from the game on the coach, I probably felt like most other Birmingham City supporters, very happy, proud of the team, but not really knowing how to react, as this is pretty much unknown territory to myself and fellow fans. To this day I still renew my season ticket annually, and attend the home games at St Andrews. My ambition for the club would always be a first FA Cup win.

CHAPTER 4

Life On Dialysis

A s I previously mentioned, transplantation was never promoted as anything other than a stopgap by the medial hierarchy at East Birmingham Hospital. The Kidney Patients' Association did try to move this forward, as we were aware of other medical opinion, such as that held by the Queen Elizabeth Hospital. We even managed to get Dr Hawkins and Tony Barnes, to attend an evening meeting, to talk to the patients about their approach to transplantation. There was no doubt that they did hold different views on the subject, and voiced their opinions to the attending audience. People who attended had to make up their own minds on the value of transplantation, after hearing both speakers. I believe both to be honest on how they individually viewed the subject, at that time. I also think they respected each other, as I did; even though their views differed.

By that time I had been asked if I wished to be put on the transplant list, and said I did. Every so often, I would receive a letter, from the hospital, asking if I wanted to remain on the list. I always responded and said, yes. I always had the feeling, whether it was something to hang onto or not, that if I received a transplant it would be successful. I understand that Dr Hawkins and his colleagues were starting to change their opinions on transplantation, and close to the end of the seventies did try to get the hospital authorities to consider building a transplant unit, at the East Birmingham Hospital, but it never materialised.

Around 1974, the Unit had started using a new artificial kidney, replacing the

Keel. The Cordis Dow as it was called, was a disposable artificial kidney. It was cylindrical, about ten inches long, and about two and half inches in diameter. Inside the cylinder, were a number of fibres, that the blood would pass through, doing the same job as the membranes in the Keel. The Cordis was used once or twice, and then disposed of. It was more efficient than the Keel, and also had the advantage of not requiring all the work surrounding the Keel; dismantling, washing, rebuilding, testing etc. The use of the Cordis was more expensive for the Unit, so they still continued the use of the Keel for most home dialysis patients. After the Cordis had been in use for a while, I decided to ask if I could be changed over to use it. This was on the basis that I was working full-time, and the slightly reduced dialysis time, and more importantly the elimination of the process surrounding the use of the Keel, would make life a lot easier, for me and my family. Doctor Hawkins readily agreed to me changing over to the Cordis, and after three years I was able to put the time consuming use of the Keel behind me.

I would attend the outpatients clinics regularly, for the usual things; blood pressure checks, blood tests and to see a doctor, this was usually Doctor Hawkins. Sometimes it would be quite a wait, as at one point everyone was given the same appointment time, however through the KPA and my general contacts, I knew many of my fellow attendees, and would converse to pass the time.

It was 1976, I had been on dialysis for four years, and I was in the outpatients clinic, sitting next to a guy who I had seen before, but did not know well. As usual in this clinic, we started a conversation. He asked me if I was on the transplant list.

"Oh yes," I replied.

"Are you sure?" he said.

"Yes, I had a letter recently, and I told them I wanted to stay on the list," I responded.

He then told me that a few days earlier he had asked to see the printout list and had found that he was not on it. He suggested that I checked to see that my name was on. After I had finished in the clinic, I made my way to the office of the Renal Unit. I knew the staff there and enquired if I was on the transplant list.

"Yes," was their response.

"Well could you just get the printout and check for me please?" I asked.

The list was produced and after looking presumably at the F's for Frazier, promptly advised, "No, you're not."

A little taken aback, I then said, "Can you get me added please?" and walked out the office.

The summer of 1976 was difficult for me. It was very hot, as you will know if you lived through it. I was working in the Purchasing Office at Alcan Plate, at that time. My Office was at the front of the one story building, with large windows. In the afternoon, the sun shone in, and with no air conditioning the heat could be unbearable. We had a thermometer, on the wall and it regularly registered 100 degrees, that summer. Very often, in mid-afternoon, I would take a walk into the factory, to get out of the heat. Even worse was the dialysis, starting about eight o'clock in the evening. I would have a fan in my bedroom, with the window open wide, but it was still hot and very uncomfortable. On a few occasions that summer, I had to curtail the dialysis in the middle of the night as I did not feel well, basically due to the fact because I was sweating, became dehydrated, reducing my blood pressure to a low level. Going to work when your blood pressure was low was not pleasant, and generally I was well pleased when the summer of 1976 had passed.

CHAPTER 5

Getting The Call

After about six years of dialysis, I was starting to have problems with getting my needles in. My veins from the fistula had pretty much had their day, and finding sites for every dialysis session was becoming harder and harder. The hospital said that I would need to have another fistula in my other arm, my right arm. Being right handed, getting needles into my right arm would be more difficult, but it was the only solution. They booked me in for my second fistula operation. I was at East Birmingham Hospital, the day before my operation, and was told it would be done under a local anaesthetic, and I could have a light breakfast before I came to the hospital. The following morning, I decided to have a fried egg on toast, for my breakfast, before I drove to the hospital. At the hospital, I was given a bed and told that they would come for me at some point in the morning, for my fistula operation. All morning, I could feel that the fried egg was hanging around, and had not been digested. About 12 noon they came for me, and I was taken to outside area of the operating theatre. The surgeon, who I had not met before came to speak to me, explaining what he was about to do, under a general anaesthetic.

He said, "You haven't had anything to eat have you?"

"Well I was told the operation was going to be under a local anaesthetic, so I had some breakfast, and I don't think it is digested properly."

Looking annoyed and after a quick discussion with the Anaesthetist, the surgeon said he only did fistulas under a general anaesthetic, so he would not be operating that day. I was wheeled off to the recovering room, without having had an operation. In an effort to get me the fistula, urgently, I was referred to a surgeon at the Queen Elizabeth Hospital. His name was Mr Mathieson, and he was willing to carry out the operation under local anaesthetic, so the operation went ahead without delay. As was the case with my first fistula, it was always going to be the case that the veins, could not be used for about six weeks after the operation. I therefore had to soldier on with the well-used veins in my left arm. In fact, I did not get to use this fistula, on my right arm, which is probably just as well because, instead of swelling the veins in my arm, it had the effect of swelling the veins in the opposite direction, in the back of my hand.

Whether it was a coincidence, or as a result of my direct contact with the transplant medical staff, at the Queen Elizabeth Hospital, six weeks after my fistula operation, I received a telephone call. It was a Wednesday evening, in September 1978, six years of dialysis behind me. In line with my usual routine, I was in bed dialysing. There was a telephone extension in my bedroom. About 10.00pm the phone rang and I answered it.

"Is that Peter?" A male voice said.

"Yes," I replied.

"This is the QE hospital, can you get yourself over here?"

"Have you got a kidney for me?"

"Yes!" was the reply.

"I am dialysing," I said.

"That's fine, just get off, and make your way to the Transplant unit, no panic," the voice advised, "See you later."

For some reason it was decided we should call a taxi, although both my sister and Dad drove. With the help of my family, I quickly got disconnected from the dialysis. When the taxi arrived the whole family, Mom, Dad, Sandra and myself piled in for the 30 minute drive to the Queen Elizabeth Hospital. When my sister had ordered the Taxi, she told them it was urgent, and gave the reason. The taxi driver advised that when he received the call, he had people in the cab, and they volunteered to get out, so it could come to us without delay.

On arrival at the hospital, we made our way to the transplant ward, and was received by the transplant co-ordinator. We were told that the kidney was on its way. I would be checked over and given a pre-med, and subject to everything being ok, the operation would go ahead, about six o'clock in the morning. My family did not need to stay, they could return home and come back the following day. I was told the kidney was a good match. There are four elements related to blood type that are matched and in this case all four matched. Recently it has become possible to carry out successful transplants, where the match is not so close. This is because techniques are available, to affect antibodies in the blood, resulting in many transplants, such as from a wife to her husband and vice versa, where the match may not be high.

The operation went ahead, and later in the morning when I woke up, I was told it went well. I was in a single room, separate from the main ward. In those days this was the practice, as they liked to keep the area as sterile as possible. All the nursing staff introduced themselves by their first names, and the atmosphere was very positive and encouraging. I was visited by the surgeon who had carried out the transplant. It turned out to have been carried out by Mr Mathieson, hopefully he had put it in the right way around! My new kidney had started working straight, away, which is not always the case, even with the successful transplants. Over the next few days visitors; relatives and friends, commented that I now had colour in my face. There was no diet restrictions or limits on fluid intake, in fact I was encouraged to drink plenty. I started to put on weight, this was food related, not fluid retention. They had taken my weight initially and I was down to 57 kgs, about nine stone, but this soon increased.

Various tests were carried out during the first few days. These included scans and X-rays, but I seemed to pass with flying colours. When there was a problem, my fellow transplantees were called up for further scans. They were collected by one of the porters. One day, one of the porters called out my name, and my heart sank. When I responded, he shouted "Can I borrow, your newspaper?"

I had only met Tony Barnes, the head of the transplant programme, a couple of times previously. He would do ward rounds like the other consultants. One morning he came into my room with a few of his junior doctors. He was his usual jovial self, and after looking at my notes he stated that everything looked to be going well. He then started looking out the window, turned and said to me, "The grass is looking a bit long down there; are you any good at mowing?"

"I'll get on to it this afternoon!" I retorted.

From the outset of the transplant, at the hospital, I was given the anti-rejection drugs used at that time. Azathioprine, a drug that reduces the effectiveness of the body's immune system by interfering with the white blood cells. The transplanted kidney is a foreign body and would be rejected without the use of this type of drug. The other drug we were given was a steroid called prednisolone. I am a lay man, in medical terms but I understand in this context, both these drugs are described as immunosuppressants. When there is a problem, such as a flu epidemic, then it is usually announced that the people at risk are the elderly the young and the immunosuppressed. A steroid, for this requirement, is used to help the body fight off any infection that it may be susceptible due to the use of the Azathioprine. Initially a high dose of the steroid is given, with the effect of making you feel hungry. As with most transplant patients, I was to develop what is called moon face, which is basically due to eating a lot, as a result of the use of the steroid. This usually lasts about six months, but does gradually go away, as the dosage of prednisolone is reduced to an on-going level.

On the tenth day after my transplant operation, half the stitches were taken out, and on the eleventh, the remaining stitches were removed, and I was allowed to go home. There is a common misconception, in terms of kidney transplant operations, many people think that one of the old kidneys is a taken out and is replaced by the donor kidney, in the same position. This is not the case, in fact, unless the original kidneys are causing high blood pressure or having some adverse effect on the body they are not removed. The donor kidney is actually inserted in the groin, and some re-plumbing is carried out by the surgeon. I was told before my release from hospital, that in the early days I would be susceptible to infection, and should avoid places where there would be a number of people for the next three months. I was also not to attend work for three months.

In the early days after the transplant, I was required to attend the outpatients clinic frequently, so any signs of rejection could be investigated and if necessary addressed quickly, this was usually by upping the anti-rejection drugs. On my first visit to outpatients, I had a high temperature, and there was concern from the medical staff, and by myself, that some rejection was occurring. After further investigation, I was advised it was not related to the transplant, but actually related to some infection from the recent fistula operation, for which antibiotics were prescribed. After this things all went one way and to all intents and purposes my health was as good as the next person, and better than many.

CHAPTER 6

The Games

I continued to be involved the Kidney Patients Association, and in the spring of 1979, the KPA were advised of something which would have a major effect on my life for the next twenty years. The QE were looking for transplant patients who would be interested in being part of the Birmingham QE team to take part in the Transplant Games, in Portsmouth that summer. As the only transplanted person on the KPA committee, at that time, I volunteered to look into it and see if I could recruit interested people. It turned out this was the second year of the Transplant Games, having been held for the first time in Portsmouth in 1978.

I discovered the Transplant Games were the idea of a transplant surgeon from St Mary's Hospital, Portsmouth. His name was Maurice Slapak, and his thinking was that if the public could see transplant patients taking part in sporting activities, it would help promote the Organ Donor Scheme, and encourage them to carry the card. Having found out more about the Transplant Games, and looking for transplanted people who came under the East Birmingham Hospital KPA, I also decided that I may be interested myself. It had been eight years since my last involvement in any physical exercise, and I was not even sure what I could achieve. However, I was always interested in sport, particularly athletics, so I thought 'why not?'. As well as athletics, I learnt that the Transplant Games also included other popular sports, such as swimming, tennis, table tennis, badminton and a few others. I thought I could at least take part in the 100 metre sprint, and maybe the sprint relay. I advised my contact at the Queen Elizabeth that I may be interested in taking part, and I was subsequently introduced to the team manager, Malcolm Simms, who was young surgeon at the Hospital working for Tony Barnes.

Malcolm was involved in sport himself. His background was in fell running, and he had thighs to prove it. He was associated with Solihull Athletics Club and regularly turned out for them in middle distance races, such as the steeplechase. He was also a really genuine, down to earth person, ideal for the team manager role, with a great sense of humour, and was also regarded as a very good surgeon. The team was quite small, but a couple of them had competed the year before.

The first fellow team member Malcolm introduced me to was Peter Ford, who had had his transplant about twelve months before I had mine. Peter had played a bit of Badminton, and Malcolm suggested we could form a Badminton doubles team. I have never been a great racket sport player, but I was willing to give it a go. Peter worked for Cadbury in Bournville, where we able to get some practise together, at their sports facility over the next few weeks. Each individual, in the Transplant Games, can enter up to five events. They can earn points for their team, usually on the basis of three points for first, two points for second, and one point for third. They would be awarded medals; gold, silver and bronze, for their achievement. The team who gained the highest number of points would be the overall team winner and would receive the team trophy. The team would usually be made up of people representing the Unit where they received their transplant, in our case, the Birmingham QE Hospital.

Although, I knew the Games had taken place, for the first time, in the previous year, I did not have an idea of the level of competition. I therefore decided, if nothing else, I needed some fitness training. I found out there was Jogging Club, across the way from my family home, and thought it could be what I was looking for. So, on a Tuesday evening, a few weeks before the Games, I made my way to the North Solihull Sports Centre, which was no more than a quarter of a mile from my house. On entering I enquired about jogging, and was told I needed to see John Walker, who ran the Jogging Club. Someone went off to find him for me. A track-suited man, in his mid-forties, I guessed, appeared and introduced himself, as John Walker. I explained my situation and said they I was interested in doing some jogging, for fitness. John said all he wanted me to do that evening, was jog the straights and walk the bends of the cindered track, at the Sports Centre, and do no more than four laps. I should also do the same on the Thursday evening, that week. Over the next few weeks, under John's instructions, I gradually built up to jogging about three miles without stopping.

Malcolm provided the team members, including myself, with a list of events, for the Games, which we could enter, and asked that we complete the form. When I looked at the list, I noticed there was a five kilometres running race, which was referred to as the Mini Marathon. Although, I could probably have completed the race, not knowing the standard, it was unlikely, given the short amount of time I had been running, that I could have been competitive. I therefore decided to enter the five mile walk, plus I entered the 100 metres, the 100 metres relay, and the Badminton doubles with Peter.

The Games were held over a long weekend. On arriving, on the Friday, we made my way down to Castle Fields, at Southsea, the seaside area of Portsmouth, where the athletic events, were to take place on the Sunday. Recognising that we were competitors, a man came over to introduce himself, his name was Brian Hall. He was one of the Games organisers, and was very friendly and welcoming. I was still concerned about the standard of competition, and wondered if I was out of my depth. This doubt was increased further when I noticed a female competitor on Castle Field, doing some exercises. She had 'Canada', on the back of her tracksuit, was tall and slim, and was going through some stretching routine which looked quite painful. If she was representative of the standard of athlete, I thought, then I was definitely out of my depth.

These Games, as had happened in the previous year, included international teams, as well the teams from Units in the UK. It was therefore quite colourful and everywhere you went you found people in their respective team colours, friendly and happy, and celebrating their new lease of life. Teams from the USA, Canada, Mexico, France, Spain, Finland, and many more countries attended. There was a team from the Republic of Ireland, resplendent in their green blazers. Their team manager was a man named Maxi Scully, who apparently had been the star of the 1978 Games, having won four gold medals for events including the 100 metres and 400 metres. Maxi was not to repeat his success at the 1979 Games, but a few years later he was to hold the world record for the highest jump by a bare back horse rider.

The timetable for my events were Saturday afternoon; Badminton, Sunday morning; five mile walk along Southsea Seafront, Sunday afternoon; at Castle Field the 100 metres, with 100 metres relay being the final event. Peter and I played a couple of games of Badminton, but did not progress to the later rounds. I did not perform well, and confirmed my earlier assessment, that I do not excel at racket sports. The next morning, I was ready for my five mile walk along Southsea seafront, finishing at Castle Field. There was a high entry, and I think some of the entrants, just viewed it as a morning stroll along the seafront. Whilst waiting for the start to commence, I managed to stand in some dog poo, maybe a lucky omen, I thought. "On your marks, go", and off we went. I settled down about halfway in the field, and gradually overtook a few people. The leaders seems to be a way ahead. As the race progressed, I thought I must be in the top dozen. I noticed a guy just in front me do a few running steps, when we were out of the view of the stewards, who were along the route, directing participants and looking at for this type of behaviour. Abiding by the rules, I still managed to overtake this individual, and was now in sight of the leaders. There were about six walkers in front of me now. I kept going with a brisk walk, and overtook another couple of people. If I could overtake the next person, I would get the bronze medal. I made a further effort and overtook him, wow! If I can keep going I've got a medal. Still feeling good, I walked as fast as I could, and the guy in second place was flagging. Soon I was in second place and the guy leading, who I later found out was Finnish, was on my radar. I overtook him, and was directed to the finishing line by a steward. Through the tape, I had won, and it was a great feeling. The stamina I gained from the jogging training, was probably a big factor in my victory.

After the walk, the QE team got together, and Malcolm advised that he had five men who had entered the 4 x 100m relay, and wanted the five of us to have a race, to decide who should be part of the relay team, and what legs they should run. We then went over to the field across the way. Measured out about 100metres, proceeded to the start, and on Malcolm's instruction off we went. I finished narrowly ahead of my other four team mates. At the end of this sprint, I felt a tightness in my thigh. Malcolm noted the positions, said the first four would be in the relay, and I would be running the final leg. As it happened, the relay team ended up as the four other racers, as I pulled up in the individual 100metres, my thigh muscle had given out, probably due to my 5-mile walk exertions in the morning.

With Southsea being a Seaside resort, and also with the efforts that had been given to advertise the event, we understood about ten thousand members of the public, would be around Castle Field to view the Sunday afternoon athletics, publicity being very much the objective of the Games. There is a large hill on the side of Castle Field which provided a natural viewing area for the public. In the early afternoon, myself and the two other walkers, who came second and third, were gathered and told to stand by the rostrum, where we would be awarded our medals. I had a chat with the guy from Finland, who was second, who said that he was he was feeling fine when I overtook him, but my walking pace was a little quicker than his. The announcement was made, and we each, in turn, climbed the rostrum to receive our medals, in front of the large crowd gathered on Castle Field hill. When I climbed on the rostrum, I threw my arms into the air, which I immediately thought was a bit over the top, but as this was the first time in my life anything like this had happened, and with what I had been through over the previously eight years, I accepted it was fair enough.

After pulling up in the 100metres, after about fifteen metres, with my thigh muscle strain, I settled down, relaxed, and watched the rest of the afternoon's proceedings. Our relay team competed but did not make the Final, and there were no more medals for the Birmingham Team. One of the races, I watched was the ladies 800metres. I spotted the girl from Canada, who I had seen on the day we arrived, doing her exercises. I was keen to see how she performed. When the starting gun was fired the other girls shot off, with the Canadian girl, almost in slow motion, following at the rear. She continued at a pace which could only be described as pedestrian. The other girls had finished the race and she still had a lap to go. Even the officials encouraged her to speed up and finish the race, as she was holding up proceedings, but they did this in a good humoured way. I subsequently found out this girl was a ballet dancer. I can only assume it was her version of the dying swan. In the evening we attended the Gala Dinner, a traditional event, which ends every Transplant Games. Malcolm excused himself, saying that he had to make a phone call to Tony Barnes to give him an update. When Malcolm returned he said that Tony sent his congratulations on my gold medal.

CHAPTER 7

Running

I continued to attend the Centurion Road Runners club, run by John Walker, after the Portsmouth Games. The club got its name because it was formed in the pub, the Centurion, which was round the corner from the Sport Centre. My Tuesday evenings, Thursday evenings, and Sunday mornings, were usually spent running round the local paths and roads with my fellow club members. Over a few months I built up to running with the main group of the club. This usually was a ten-mile run on a Tuesday and Thursday evening, and sometimes a little further on Sunday morning. The location of the North Solihull Sports Club was good for running, in that it was close to the countryside, where Coleshill was a regular part of the route, in the summer, and in the winter the built up areas of Sheldon and Castle Bromwich, provided well lit roads. Within the main group, you were still able to run at your own pace. It was a case of being at the front, middle or back, I was usually at the rear. Otherwise you would find a few people of similar pace, form your own group, and go out on one of the regular routes that was mutually agreed prior to the start. I soon found my own small group of people to run with.

One of my regular running mates was Steve Price, who had started running about the same time as myself. Steve had previously belonged to a swimming club and regularly competed in swimming competitions. Steve decided he needed a new challenge, which was probably influenced by the fact that club swimmers were getting younger, and more difficult to compete against. Over a period of time, my training run times gradually reduced to a point where for the regular ten miles my time would be around seventy minutes. Tuesday and Thursday evenings would usually pan out as follows; 7.00 pm arrive at the Sports Centre, 7.20pm start 10-mile run with fellow group members, 8.30pm finish run, warm down and a few stretching exercises, followed by a shower, leave Sports Centre about 9pm, for home or a local pub with running mates. With other club members, I would take part in the local ten mile races organised by the well-known Athletics clubs in the West Midlands, such as Birchfield, Tipton and Solihull, under 3A's rules (Amateur Athletics Association). I would achieve times of about sixty-three minutes in these races, compared with the winning times which would be about forty-six/seven minutes. We would also take part in shorter races. The earliest that I can remember, having not long joined the Jogging Club, was at Hyde Park, where they had established an event made up of a series of 5k (3.1 miles) runs. There were a number of runs with categories related to age and sex. As my running was in its early days, I was grateful it was a downhill course. I had been running for a year or so, when I took part in a relay race, held at the Silverstone Race Track. The track is just over three miles long. Centurion entered three relay teams, with six runners in a team, each runner covering a lap. Steve and I were in the third team, which was thrown together of who wanted to go and who was left after the first two teams had been selected. Steve was to run last, as the quickest amongst our team. I took the second leg and ran as hard as I could on what was quite a pleasant surface to run on, although conditions were difficult due to a strong wind. I handed over to our next runner and off he went. We knew that we were not going to break any records, but keen to perform as best we could. Our team member, on that leg came into view, on the far side of the track. Steve and I could not believe our eyes when we observed he was running backwards.

"What the hell is he doing?" exclaimed Steve, and we both shook our heads.

After he finished and passed on to our next runner. We questioned him as to why he was running backwards, all he could come up with was that it was windy over there! If I tell people I once went round Silverstone in nineteen minutes, I usually get a puzzled look. It was also the time of the emergence of mass marathons in this country. Chris Brasher had been inspired by the New York Marathon and turned his idea of a marathon in London, into a reality in 1981. However, the year before, John Walker, with the help of members of the Centurion club, put on a mass marathon, around Chelmsley Wood, the location of the North Solihull Sports Centre. The course was made up of three eight mile laps with the addition of start and finish sections, making the marathon distance of 26 miles and 385 yards. As I heard a few times in the future, "If it wasn't for the Royal Family, we would not have to do this 385 yards!"

This referred to the fact that prior to 1908, the specified marathon distance was 26 miles. When the Olympics were held in London, in 1908, the original finish for the 26 miles, was changed, so the finish, in the stadium, could be in front of the Royal Box, an additional 385 yards. This has been the traditional distance ever since. John called his marathon, the Peoples' Marathon, indicating that it was for the masses, not just for elite runners, the basic philosophy of the London Marathon.

I, along with other members of the club, and other friends of John, helped, as required, in the weeks leading up to the first Peoples' Marathon, in 1980. During the weekend the Marathon was run, there was a lot to do, and everyone worked extremely hard. This included the erection of hundreds of barriers, at the start and finishing areas, roping off areas, setting up chairs and tables, for reception areas in the Marquees, plus many other tasks including car parking, etc. On the day itself, along with John's father-in-law, I had the task of sorting out the water supply to the drinks stations, which were to be manned by volunteers such as Scout Groups. As an 'official', with the sign in the front of my car to prove it, John's father-in-law and myself were able to drive around, during the run, to sort any problems, if we could. Alternatively we would report to the 'central control', by the use of a radio, when necessary. At the end of a long and exhausting day, we were loading up metal barriers onto trailers, dismantling everything that we could, and generally cleaning up so the area would be back to normal for the Monday morning. It was a successful first marathon. Well supported and enjoyed, if that is the word, by the participants and to be repeated the following year. We also raised some money for charity, with the money going to 'Sailing for the disabled'.

The Transplant Games in 1980, were to be held in Birmingham, and organised by the Queen Elizabeth Hospital. Tony Barnes was the Chairman of the QE Games organisation, with Malcolm Simms being one of the main organisers. The Portsmouth committee, lead by Maurice Slapak, had decided that, after organising the Games for the first two years, they wanted to have, what would be domestic games, organised annually by different units around the country, and Birmingham had offered.

The first two Games, in Portsmouth, had been open to foreign countries, who would have their own domestic games, and from the performances at these games would select a team to represent their country, at the international games. New York were very keen to be the first international venue, following Portsmouth, and it was agreed that the New York games would be held in September 1980. Not all countries, with transplant programmes, at that time held domestic games, but those who did not made their own arrangements for selecting their team.

I decided not to include 100metres, in my events, as this could have an adverse affect, on my main races. Although, I was keen to run in the relay, as I like being part of a team, and the relays were generally the last event of the games. Everyone was allowed to take part in five events. I thought I might as well try something else, apart from racket sports, as if I did well it would be scoring for the team. Swimming was being on the Saturday afternoon, all my other event were on Sunday. I could not get injured swimming, could I? I was not a strong swimmer, in fact, the breast stroke, was the only stroke I could do. I managed a bit of swimming training so I would at least be able to compete in the shorted breast stroke event, one length of the pool.

Although called the Birmingham Games, the majority of the sporting venues were in Solihull. So in the summer of 1980, on a Saturday afternoon, I found myself in Tudor Grange Swimming Pool, Solihull about to compete in a swimming race. I questioned my sanity, bearing in mind my swimming ability, but I was there, swimming for the team, and I needed to get on with it. One thing I had not practised was diving in, which apart from the backstroke event was quite an important element of swimming races. The pistol went off, and I duly dived in. When I surfaced all of the other swimmers were well ahead of me, and well into their stokes. I did as well as I could but finished well behind everyone, to the sympathetic applause of spectators. It has always been something of a tradition at the Transplant Games that the person who comes last gets the same applause as the winners. This is because friends, relatives, and other spectators, understand that people who take part in the games all have their own individual stories. Some have struggled with their health from childhood and after transplantation, they were able to participate, in sporting completion, which made them winners, wherever they finished. In my case, that day, I did not think the applause was justified.

The following morning the mini-marathon was to be staged around Tudor Grange Park, with the Tudor Grange track, being used for the races in the afternoon. The track was managed by Pat Cropper, she and her husband Dave Cropper, had both been international athletes in their younger days and had been part of the sports organising team for the Birmingham Games, through their association with Malcolm Simms.

From running five kilometres, before, I knew my capability at this event and the pace necessary to run to suit my ability. As the race started I moved away in front, but was soon joined by another runner, who seemed comfortable at my speed. As the race progressed we were still running together, and were someway ahead of the runners behind us. We had been going for about two miles, I was feeling comfortable, but still had my rival, who I later found out was guy named Paul West, running alongside me. I decided to test him, and made a short spurt, he responded and after 40–50 yards, we returned to our previous pace. About half a mile later, I tried the same again, with the same result. We were getting near to the finish and Paul gradually upped the pace. I was struggling and was unable to keep up with him, he carried on to win the race comfortably and I was second. I talked to Paul afterwards. He was the team manager of the Liverpool team and was a transplant patient, but in the absence of anyone from the Hospital to be team manager he had taken up the mantle and organised the team. But as team manager he was non scoring, which seemed to be strange, as he was one of their likely scorers. Paul told me he found my attempts to shake him off a couple of times in the race quite funny, and we both laughed.

In the afternoon I lined up for the 1,500 metres race, with another lad from the Birmingham team, named Paul. Three and three-quarter laps of the Tudor Grange track, was in front of us. As the race settled down there were a few runners, including myself and Paul, close together. After the first lap some of the runners fell behind, with Paul and myself pulling away. Dave Cropper was commentating and during the second lap he stated that the two Birmingham lads were well in front. I was in the lead, and as the third lap progressed Paul started to fall away, and I entered the last lap well in front, and basically all I needed to do was trot home. As I was entering the final straight, the crowd were becoming very noisy, which I put down to the fact that majority would be local and supporting a local representative victory, so I carried on with my trot to the finish. I was about a yard from the finishing line, when out of the blue, a runner passed me to win the race. He fell down just after the line trying to get his breath back. What the crowd were trying to tell me, but in my naivety as a novice track racer I was misinterpreting, was that there was a guy speeding up behind me about to overtake. He had apparently run the last lap like a 400 metre runner. I made a mental note never to let this happened to me again, and be aware of what was happening behind me. The guy who overtook me was from the Sheffield Unit, his name was John Copley. I did encounter him again, with varying outcomes.

As they called for my medal presentation for the mini-marathon, later in the afternoon, I was announced as the gold medallist, and the silver, and bronze, were awarded to the third and forth finishes, respectively. I was confused, but it turned out that as Paul West had put himself down as Team Manager, he was not officially part of the team, and was basically competing as a guest, and therefore was not entitled to any points for his team, or the medal. Paul, promptly went off home, very displeased, and I had a lot of sympathy for him. As far as I was concerned I had two seconds, at the Birmingham Games, although I was annoyed with myself that I did not win the 1,500 metre race, that I was awarded the silver medal for.

Whether this was enough to get me selected for the international team, to represent Great Britain in New York later that year, I doubted, but tried to blank this question out of my mind. Over the Games weekend in Birmingham, we were aware of some filming going on by the BBC. Certain people had been interviewed including Tony Barnes. One of the people I recognised interviewing, was David Icke. He was then a young reporter for the BBC, having recently retired from professional football, having played in goal for Coventry. He is now better known for his somewhat weird views, about royalty, etc. I knew some film had been shot of the end of the mini marathon, and although personally that was the point I was struggling, I was still looking forward to seeing some Games footage on the BBC, within the next few days, with the resulting good publicity for the Organ Donor Scheme. A few weeks went by and nothing was shown on the BBC, and so like most other people involved, I forgot about it. A few months later, the BBC publicised a *Panorama* programme, they were to show, which concerned transplantation. Like many others I was horrified by the programme. It purported to say that organs were being taken from people who were not dead, doctors were only interested in taking the organs and were not carrying out proper checks on prospective donors, etc. They were using footage taken at the Birmingham Games, as background film for the programme. All of their insinuations were soon discredited, but it did damage the transplant programme at that time. It is probably unfair to the recent producers of *Panorama* programmes, but I always view the programmes they produce with scepticism after their distasteful programme, in 1980.

CHAPTER 8

The Letter

A couple of weeks after the Birmingham Games, we went off on a family holiday. On my return, there was a letter for me. It looked official and I was hoping it was what I thought it might be. I carefully opened it, and read, 'Dear Peter, Congratulations, you have been chosen to represent Great Britain, in the Transplant Olympics, in New York, in September...etc.'

"Yes!" I exclaimed. It was a great feeling, I don't think any correspondence before or since has ever come up to this, the first time I was advised that I would be representing Great Britain. The letter was signed by Pat Cropper, who was appointed British Team Manager, with her experience as an international athlete. Malcolm was also included in the management team, and had also been part of the selection committee, Pat's husband, Dave Cropper, was also lending his experience to the British Team, and travelling to New York.

A team get together had been arranged at Tudor Grange track where everyone could be informed of the arrangements for New York. Things like paperwork, including entry forms, travel arrangements, and being measured up for team tracksuits and sportswear, were attended to. As with the domestic transplant games, there is a requirement for the world games, that everyone taking part had a recent blood test, with blood pressure, etc., where the results were recorded, on a form signed by the Unit doctor. If the results were found to be outside certain set limits, an individual would be refused permission to participate in the games.

The British team was made up of about twenty people. When I had a chance, I asked Malcolm how they had made the selection. He told me that they had selected people who had come first in a minimum of one event, and also people were selected where they had come second in two or more events. Hence, as I had been second in two events, they had given me a place in the team. Paul West who had beaten me in the mini marathon, had also been selected. Although he had not received the gold medal, for a technical reason, it was recognised that he had satisfied the criteria for being selected.

The team flew from Heathrow Airport, to New York's John F. Kennedy Airport. I travelled to the airport with Pat and Dave Cropper, as we all lived in the Solihull area. We were accommodated at the Holiday Inn on Sixth Avenue in New York, not far from Central Park. The Holiday Inn at that time was certainly past its best, but the room we had was large, and had three beds. It turned out that I was sharing with Paul West and also a younger lad named John Murray. Paul had not been able to attend the get together at Tudor Grange, but had been asked who he wanted to share with and he had put myself down, as I was the only name he recognised. John Murray was about twenty at the time. He was a bubbly character, a likeable lad, but was liable to do the wrong thing on occasions that could get him into trouble. He annoyed Paul a few times, and insisted on calling Paul, 'Salmon', something to do with Paul West's middle name being John!

We were warned against walking round certain areas of New York at night, which at that time, in the days before Mayor Rudy Giuliani had introduced 'Zero Tolerance', were considered dangerous. We also heard, on the floor below us, in the Hotel itself, there had been a recent shooting. With a few other lads from the team, we went out one night, and thought we would go into a club, although it looked a little dubious. Once inside we realised it was probably run by the mafia, and after one drink made a quick exit, when one of the lads, heard something on the lines of, "What are these schmucks doing in here?" from one of the girls.

The opening ceremony consisted of a short procession along Sixth Avenue and into Central Park, where we had a few speeches and a barbeque. I believe New York was bankrupt at that time and some of the venues would go along with that. For those of us who were taking part in the track events, we were bussed off to the dilapidated home of the New York Cosmos Soccer Team, who I think were temporarily out of action, at the time. It was like a concrete jungle, to say the least. We were then told that the 1,500 metres, would not be a race, but we were to run the distance individually, and this would be timed. So our race was basically a time trial. We questioned this, but that was the way it was going to be organised. As well as being time consuming, and boring for people watching, it meant that you had to run as hard as possible, with no one to measure your pace against. Unfortunately, this seemed to be typical of the New York organisation. At the end of the individual runs in the 1,500metres, my time was third quickest, and at least I would be receiving the bronze medal, but not in a satisfactory way.

The winner of the gold was a runner from Finland, and the silver was going to my rival from Sheffield, John Copley, who had beaten me to the tape in Birmingham in the 1,500 metres. We had both contributed to the medal table, for our GB team. Paul West had been struggling with a knee injury, and wore a knee support. He had competed in this time trial but was obviously having problems, and further aggravated it, which ruled him out of any further competition. Between competing, Paul, John, and myself spent most of our time walking round New York looking for sports shops. This was initiated by Paul as he wanted to buy some trainers, knowing they were cheaper in the US. I think Paul was determined to visit every sports shop in New York, and John and I followed him like lemmings. After a few hours of walking miles, both John and I started to get a bit fed up, and made a few comments to Paul. He would respond with something like, "Oh, I'm sure there's a sports shop at the bottom of this road".

I recall we went into a New York Café, and thought we would try the local fayre, so we ordered three 'banana splits'. We could not believe it when they came and each banana split contained six bananas. One between us would have easily been enough for our needs. The venues and organisation of the New York games, continued in the same vain, apart from the five kilometres (mini-marathon) event, which had been handed over to the New York Road Runners' Club, who organise the New York Marathon. They did an excellent job in putting on this event. The race was held in Central Park, with proper start and finish areas, drinks stations, distance markers each kilometre and was well stewarded. There was a good entry for the race, on a warm day, I stood at the start ready to compete. I recognised the tall Finish runner, who had the fastest time in the 1,500 metres and thought he would be the main guy, which proved to be right. In front of us was a downhill section of about 300 hundred yards, before it levelled out, and as it was a turn around course there would be an uphill finish.

As the pistol went off for the start a few runners went off like express trains and although I did not want to be left behind I knew that at that pace they would soon tire, so I kept to the speed I was comfortable at. One of the runners who went off really fast was an Australian lad. He seems to be treating the race like a 400 hundred metres. As I continued with my comfortable pace, I was starting to overtake some of the runners who had bombed the first few hundred yards. After about 600 yards, I came across the Australian runner learning up against an official's van, looking exhausted, I was not surprised. If he had run five kilometres before, he certainly had not learned from the experience. After about a mile and a half I overtook another runner, it was my British Team mate from Sheffield, John Copley, who had won the silver in the 1,500 metres. I was comfortable and he was obviously out of his comfort zone, at that point. I acknowledged him, as I overtook. The course was set up so there was a turn round at the half way point and the return route was on the other side of the road, in Central Park. At this point there were four runners in front of me, and I could see the flying Fin was well in front. I started to make progress and in wasn't long before I was in third place. With about a kilometre to go I had the runner who was in second place in sight. I later found out he was Dutch, and was an international athlete, who represented Holland, prior to his kidney problems and subsequent transplant. The Finnish runner was out of sight, but I was intent on trying to catch the second place runner, and I was gaining ground on him. As I overtook him, I could see he was struggling, and would not be able to respond, and I carried on up the hill to the finish, to take the silver.

The ladies race was also taking place within the same run, and a few minutes later I was happy to see our British lady runner, Angela Dunn, take silver, in her race. Great Britain had another two silver medals to add to the medal table. Our team photographer, Gordon White, took a photograph of Angela and myself, at the end of mini marathon, in Central Park, both happy with our silver medals for GB.

Another unbelievable part of the New York organisation, concerned the awarding of medals. For some inexplicable reason they had decided not to present the medals at the sport venues themselves, but to present all the medals at the end of games Gala Dinner prior to the meal. The Gala Dinner was held in a large room, at one of the New York Hotels. At the start of the evening all the medal recipients, including myself, were gathered together and matched onto the stage area, to be awarded the medals. Apart from being ready to eat and fighting off hunger pains, the assembled throng, spent the next hour being bored to death whilst the medals were awarded for each event of the games. After this it was announced that the British team had won the greatest number of medals, and therefore had won the team award, our team captains, Dave Davies and Annabel Johnson, went up to receive the trophy. Amongst other good performances were the 100 metres gold for Dave Lawrenson, an event which had a large entry, and our swimming team, which included some excellent swimmers. Needless to say the swimming team did not include myself. When we arrived back at Heathrow, newspaper photographers were present. Wearing British team tracksuits, with the individual medal around our necks, we were happy to be snapped. Again we hoped that our efforts would, as well giving us great satisfaction, would be good publicity for the Organ Donor Scheme.

CHAPTER 9

The Management Committee

Shortly after the New York Games, I was contacted by Malcolm, who advised me that the Portsmouth Committee, with Maurice Slapak at the helm, had decided they should form a management committee, to be the governing body of the Transplant Games in this country. Tony Barnes and Malcolm had been invited to be part of this, and the Portsmouth group were also looking for a couple of transplant recipients to join the committee. He told me that he and Tony would like to put my name forward, if I was interested. I told him I would be and he said he would be in touch. Shortly afterwards, I was off to a meeting in Portsmouth, accompanying Tony Barnes and Malcolm, at which the Transplant Olympic Association of Great Britain, was formed. Maurice Slapak was voted in as Chairman, and amongst others on the committee was Brian Hall, as an administrator. Brian worked for Portsmouth Council and he was the man who welcomed me to the Portsmouth Games on the first day. Orien Young, who had represented Barbados in the 100 metres sprint at the Olympics, was the sports expert and coach. David Oliver who was a solicitor, and legal advisor. Mike Whiteside, was a kidney transplant recipient, a very good badminton player who had a naval background, and ran a marina near Portsmouth. Also on the committee was a lady transplant surgeon, from Liverpool. Her name was Chris Evans, a remarkable person who smoked cigars, drank pints and had a number of interests, including rowing. Tony Barnes and Malcolm would also be included in the original members of the Committee. The original aims of the Portsmouth organisation, in terms of publicity for organ donation, would form part of the constitution of the management committee. The Transplant Olympic Association of Great Britain, would also be responsible for accepting bids from the Transplants Units, up and down the country, to run the annual domestic games and award them to the Units where appropriate. In the following months, and years, I took on the role of membership secretary for the 'TOAGB'.

Initially this was voluntary for people who wished to compete in the Transplant Games, but eventually it was decided to make this mandatory. The initial annual fee was only two pounds, but it would cover the cost of Newsletters, and other correspondence, that was send out directly to members. The committee felt that the membership secretary's role would be best carried out by a transplant patient, because of the relationship with fellow transplantees. It was also useful that the newsletters were to be jointly produced by Malcolm and myself, living close to each other. Malcolm had the biggest input into the newsletters, and his sense of humour produced some memorable editions.

CHAPTER 10

Marathon Time

The next Peoples' Marathon would be in May 1981, and number of runners from the Centurion Club, including myself, let John Walker know that they would like to run the marathon for the first time in that event. John accepted this but was concerned he would be short of helpers. Those of us who helped previously, and a few others, committed themselves to help, as best as we could before and after the marathon. The entry was going to be larger than the first year, so one of the things that John needed help with was the administrative side. In those days, before personal computers became a common item in most households, all the entries came in by letter to John's house, which was about 100 yards from the entrance to the Sport Centre. John enlisted a few people to help with the admin side, of which I was one. When John and his family were away on holiday he especially needed the entry forms to be dealt with so there would not be a mountain of letters on his return. I was one of a rota of a people doing this. I recall coming out of work at lunchtime, going to John's house, picking up all the post, opening, recording, filing cheques etc., as necessary.

Steve and I discussed our training for the marathon. Our weekly mileage was usually between thirty and thirty five miles. We would do ten miles on Tuesday and Thursday, and on Sunday a little further, maybe twelve miles. For our marathon training, we would need to up this to about fifty miles a week, at least for the three months prior to the event. The emphasis would be on gradually increasing the distance of the Sunday morning run, eventually up to twenty miles, which would be the longest we would do in training prior to the marathon. We would also introduce a Saturday run, and lengthen our Tuesday and Thursday runs by a couple of miles. This had to be done gradually, as we knew that injuries would only put things back. Such things as shin splints are common if mileage is increased too quickly. This was unknown territory to us. Something that we had never done before and we didn't even know whether we could do it. We intended to do a few twenty mile runs in training, near to the event, but we were also told that twenty miles is the halfway point in a marathon. The basic point is that the last six miles and 385 yards, feels like another twenty miles, as the weariness kicks in. We also heard about the 'wall', as it was called, which could occur after eighteen miles, a point where your energy could be exhausted.

True to our word, we committed ourselves to help John where we could, with the marathon organisation. One day, Steve, myself, and another running mate of ours, were cornered by John, with the slightly worrying words of, "I've got just the job for you three."

The 1981 route was changed from the previous year, to a one lap course. To do this John was incorporating part of the then unused, but soon to be opened M42, and the Collector Road, which ran parallel to the M6, near Chemsley Wood. The three mile section of the M42, which John intended to use, was in need of some attention, in that there were glass, nails, and various other rubbish on it, which could make it a little hazardous for marathon runners. John had decided we were the right calibre of 'plonkers' for this very important task, and said he would supply the brooms for sweeping the three mile section. I don't think we could believe it ourselves, when we were carrying out this task, but John was a persuasive character, and nothing that he came up with surprised me. Another example of this was the night before the marathon, when another worrying statements to myself and some Ranger Scouts, who were helping, came out of John's mouth, "I have got a clandestine mission for you!".

John then explained that there was a wire fence that needed to be dismantled. The fence ran between the side of the Sports Centre and the main road. The approach to the finish was alongside the Sports Centre, and unless to wire mesh of the fence was removed runners would have to detour to the pavement or road, which was not ideal. John knew that the council might baulk at dismantling the fence, so he decided, on this undercover action, late at night in the dark. The Ranger Scouts and yours truly, were handed the tools for the job, and carried out the clandestine operation as instructed. The fence would be made good after the marathon, and it would be almost as good as before we dismantled it.

Our training had been going pretty well, and we had been achieving our fifty miles a week, which was the plan. Six weeks before the marathon we ran our first twenty mile training run. We incorporated two of our usual ten mile routes so we were certain of the distance. It took us about two and a half our hours. I was tired at the end, but reasonably happy with the way it went. We repeated this four weeks before the marathon, and also two weeks before the event, and were generally happy with these runs. For the week of the marathon itself, we were advised to take it easy. With this in mind we reduced the week's running to about fifteen miles, and tried to ensure a good 'pasta' intake the day before.

It was Sunday 10th May, 1981, my thirty-first birthday, and I was about to undertake my first marathon. Malcolm was also running, as I had got him an entry form, when he told me he would liketo run the marathon. Malcolm, was a strong runner, who would plod the return journey from his home to the hospital daily, adding to his competitive runs for the Solihull Athletics Club. My plan was to run my own race. I knew that Steve was quicker than me, so I would not try to stay with him, which could hold him back, or push myself too hard early on. I would run the first five miles at an easy pace just to get into my running. After that I should be into my running, and thought the training would let me know that I was not running too fast for the early part of the race. This proved to be correct. I was passing the mile signs 10, 12, 15, taking on regular water, as advised, and things were going well. After about twenty miles, the course was close to Coleshill, and I remember feeling good as I overtook a couple of the lads from the running club. They looked like they were slowing down somewhat, probably as a result of going a little too fast early on. The Collector Road was about three miles long. About half way along I saw the twenty three miles sign, I was starting to feel a little weary. I was a running alongside a girl, and had a chat which helped take my mind off the effort of keeping going. I asked her if this was her first marathon, and she said that she had run one before, and was confident of finishing. Just after that I pushed on leaving her behind with the end in sight. I went through the finishing line and was ushered into one of the finish funnels by one of the stewards. Someone put a medal over my head, and another person handed me a Mars bar, which I promptly ate. My time was three hours, 12 minutes, and 58 seconds, which I was happy with. I had not given too much thought to the time that I would achieve prior to the race, it was more about would I be able to complete a marathon, and I had answered that question.

The following evening the phone rang and it was Malcolm. He apologised for not stopping to see me finish the race, but had needed to get away promptly, after he finished. He asked me how I had got on, and when I told him my time he sounded impressed, and surprised. I think he thought it would be more like four or five hours. He said he would be contacting Tony Barnes, who he was certain would want to get some publicity from my run. Malcolm's time had been around two hours 45 minutes. He said he enjoyed the event, it had gone well for him, and he thanked me for getting him an entry. The following morning at work, I was contacted by a reporter from the *Birmingham Evening Mail*, who took some details, over the phone, and arranged for me to meet a photographer, who would be taking some pictures of me in my running gear. That evening the article appeared in the *Birmingham Evening Mail*, and read as follows:-

'Birmingham marathon man Peter Frazier is the pride and joy of top surgeon Tony Barnes today, after becoming the first kidney transplant recipient to complete the gruelling 26 miles course. Three years ago, Peter was spending hours a week on a dialysis machine at his home in Denise Drive, Kingshurst. But the former policeman, who had to give up his job, when kidney disease struck, 10 years ago, was in great form when he celebrated his 31st birthday, on Sunday. And he crossed the Chelmsley Marathon finish line only 44 minutes after the leader, with more than a thousand competitors still behind him.'

There were two other local marathons that summer, and I took the opportunity to take part in both. The training I had done for the People's marathon would provide a good platform for these two runs. The next marathon was called the 'Brum Run', which I think was organised by a commercial outfit. This marathon would start at the NEC (National Exhibition Centre) near Birmingham Airport. The route would then be into the City Centre, then back out via Solihull, and back into the NEC finish point. Between the Peoples marathon and the 'Brum Run', I had gone on holiday, and certainly had taken the opportunity to take things easy for a couple of weeks. After coming back, about two weeks prior to the 'Brum Run', I decided I needed a long run, to check my fitness, and to get me back into training. Off I went on a twenty mile training run, which seems to go pretty well.

It was the day of the 'Brum Run', and I lined up with the masses to head for Birmingham City Centre. It was a pretty hot day, and I kept well hydrated around the route. We went through Solihull, heading for Catherine De Barnes, where we would turn left and head towards the NEC. I was struggling, but kept going as best as I could and finished in a time of three hours and seven minutes. The Brum Run organisers, came up with an electronic system of clocking in at the finish, as a recording device. I have not seen this system before or since. The runners were given these cardboard 'clock in cards', before the race. At the finish you were asked to clock in, as if you were in a factory. I did as instructed, but was most disappointed when I checked in the local paper to see that it had not registered my time. I had worked out my position in the race would be about 200th, but my name was nowhere to be seen.

At the end of People's Marathon, apart from feeling a little tired, I felt pretty good. At the end of the Brum Run, I felt decidedly off, and had to sit down for a while, in the Marquee. Once I got a hot sweet drink down me, I was soon up and ready to make my way home. The 'Brum Run' was never to be staged again. The Police would have opposed the route being used again, as they had many complaints, regarding road closures across the City, and into the City Centre. Police generally are against circular routes for marathons, because of the traffic problems they cause. It was surprising that the 'Brum Run', got permission for the route it had, in the first place. I think, also, that the commercial outfit that ran it, may have decided that it was not a good investment.

The third marathon that summer was the 'Sandwell Marathon'. Sandwell is a district that borders Birmingham, on the Northern side. The marathon was organised by Sandwell Council. The start was in an industrial part of Sandwell, but also took in some of the park areas in the region. After about sixteen miles, the course took to the pavement of Birmingham Road, which was a very steep hill, for about a mile and a half. I managed to keep going but it did seem to take something out of me, but close to the end of the race I felt my pace was quite reasonable and I finished in good shape. My time was three hours and seven minutes, and this time it was properly recorded, and confirmed that was pretty much my optimum time.

CHAPTER 11

Transplant Games 1981

My marathons out the way for that year, my concentration now returned to the Transplant Games. The International Games were every two years, so the domestic games did not involve international selection in 1981, that would be the following year. The Games in 1981 were hosted by the Manchester Unit. Malcolm asked me if I would take over as team manager, for the Birmingham team, as he had other commitments, but he was also looking at this as a long term role. Team Managers were responsible for organising their team, circulating the entry forms etc. At the start of each games, there was usually a Team Managers' Meeting, where representatives of the organising committee would inform team managers, of any specific things they should be aware of, or needed to pass onto their team. As a member of the TOAGB management committee, I needed to attend another meeting, as we would take advantage of the games weekend to hold one of our meetings.

These would sometimes be on a Sunday morning, which could clash with my five kilometre run, but I just had to work round it, and my run would take priority. On the Friday evening, and Saturday of the Manchester games, I ran into a few of the British team members, who had been, in New York, with me. This included a few from Manchester, who had been well represented in New York. Knowing that I was a middle distance runner, a couple of the Manchester guys mentioned that one of their team had competed in the Manchester Marathon, that summer. His name was Patrick Murphy. I had to advise that I had had some marathon activity myself, that summer. 'It looked like there could be some interesting races that weekend', I thought.

The mini-marathon, was staged on the Sunday morning, and would start in the Athletic stadium. There would be two laps of the course, outside the stadium, and then back in the stadium at the end for the finish. We were advised there would be a hare, who was pointed out to us. This guy was a runner from the local Athletic Club, who would run in front of us, to make sure we went the right way. We were assembled on the track, behind the start line, with our hare in front, and the starter gave his instruction and fired the gun. I went off in front, not too far behind the hare, and followed him round the track and out of the stadium. With the amount of running I had done over the previous months, I was confident of the pace I could do, and knew what I could maintain. Over the first lap of the course, with the hare in front regularly checking he was in my sight, I was not aware of anyone close behind me. At the start of second lap, I was sure someone was near me and shortly after there was another runner alongside me. It was Patrick Murphy, who I knew by sight, but had not been introduced to. I quickened up a little and Patrick kept alongside me. About half way round the second lap, I decided to try a burst of speed, and see what happened. My previous experience of doing this, when running against Paul West, had been a bit of a farce, but this was another day and another runner. Patrick responded to my surge and we settled down to running side by side again.

We were close to returning to the stadium, so I decided on another surge, but this time I would sustain it longer, and see what happened. Again Patrick responded, but as I maintained it, he started to fall back, and I opened a gap. As I ran onto the track, I was about fifty yards in front of him, which was enough for me to go on and win the race. At the end of the run, I shook hands with Pat and we had a chat. Pat was a nice guy, and I always found him to be a gutsy runner, whenever we ran against each other. We also had a chat with the hare. He told us that he had not expected the standard to be that high, and was surprised we had both run marathons. In the afternoon we lined up at the start of the 1,500 metres, on the track, along with some other runners. It was a similar scenario, as the morning. I went off in front and until the final lap, when I felt someone close behind, which I assumed was Pat. The other reason I knew I was being pursued, and by Pat, was because the crowd, predominantly from Manchester, were making a lot of noise, encouraging their man, and they were getting louder by the second. As I came round the final bend into the straight, I lapped a runner, and as I overtook this guy, I accelerated and sprinted to the finish, without easing up. I was not trying to show off, or humiliate Pat, I just wanted to make sure I won the race. I was never going to let what happened to me in Birmingham happen again. Pat finished about fifteen yards behind me, he just gave it everything he had, in front of his home crowd, which I expected of him. I was talking to a few of my fellow games competitors, after the race. One of them was a young girl swimmer from Manchester, Frances Hilton, who had been one of our stars of the pool in New York, "Didn't yer go!", she exclaimed in a Mancunian accent.

CHAPTER 12

What About The Day Job?

As I mentioned earlier, in 1973, I had taken up a position as Assistant Buyer at Alcan Plate. They had been taken over by the Alcan Group, 'Alcan' being the Aluminium Company of Canada, who competitors would be 'Baco' (as in BACO foil) British Aluminium Company, and 'Alcoa', Aluminium Company of America. Alcan Plate at Kitts Green, was a specialist aluminium plate producer. 'Plate' was the thicker aluminium, which could be something like three to six inches thick. Then there was 'Sheet' which was probably up to about half an inch thick, and in between was 'Shate' (this was the technical term for it). The plate produced at Kitts Green, was used for aircraft manufacture, and also for defence vehicles, tanks etc. When I started work there, in 1973, there were about 1,300 employees, and it was a 24-hour operation, with a three shift manufacturing system. The Buying office itself, consisted of a Supplies Manager, a Chief Buyer, a Buyer, Assistant Buyer and a couple of Admin/Typists.

The Supplies Manager, Charlie Smart, was in overall control of the buying, and the purchase of Aluminium ingot, and other metals, was handled by him directly. Charlie Smart, was a white haired man in his sixties, who had worked for the company as long as anyone could remember. He rarely came out of his office, but it was always said that he had his finger on the pulse of the Company. His number two was Eric Walker, a smart man in his fifties who had had a military background. Eric basically ran the Buying Office on a day-to-day basis.

I generally got on well with both these gentlemen and was happy with my working life. I don't think it was as a result of my employment, but after about a year, working at Alcan Plate, the hierarchy, decided to reduce the work force from 1,300 to around 900, and various redundancy initiatives were put forward to the workforce. This was not a great time for moral generally, with unions and management at loggerheads, but eventually things settled down, and the workforce had been reduced to the required level. Charlie Smart, at this time, let it be known that he intended to retire shortly, with the intention that Eric would replace him. Eric advised me one day, that Charlie and himself, had been pleased with my work, and they were promoting me to Buyer. Eric suffered with high blood pressure, which he took tablets for. He was also careful with his diet, to control his cholesterol level, and would usually put his feet up at lunchtime, again to help with his blood pressure. Just before Charlie was due to retire, Eric had visited his doctor, where he had discussed his imminent promotion to Supplies Manager. Suspecting this post would bring extra stress to his working life, with the background of Eric's health, his Doctor had recommended he declined the post. Reluctantly Eric accepted the doctor's advice, and informed senior management of his decision.

Charlie Smart's replacement, was Roger Jones, who came up from the Company's factory in Newport, South Wales. Roger would be in his thirties, a proud Welshman, whose cousin, Bobby Windsor, was part of the famous Pontypool front line and a regular Welsh Rugby Union international. As time progressed Roger was keen that I should get some purchasing qualifications, and was willing to give me some time off to help with this. After leaving school at sixteen with three GCE 'O' levels, Maths, Art, and Technical Drawing, and a few CSEs, I had not had any further education. My intention was always to join the police force, when I was nineteen, so I did not pursue additional education. The main qualification for Buyers, was the 'Institute of Purchasing and Supply'. Now known as the 'Chartered Institute of Purchasing and Supply' (CIPS). I found out that if I took the 'Higher National Certificate' (HNC) in Business

Studies, a two year course, incorporating the Purchasing subject, I would then only need to take the final year of the 'Purchasing and Supply' course, to achieve the qualification. I was able to go straight to HNC, without gaining ONC (Ordinary National Certificate), as I was over 26. In 1977, I attended Aston Polytechnic, near the centre of Birmingham, for the two year HNC in Business Studies Course. I was given the afternoon off work, with the course day, taking in the evening at the Polytechnic. (Aston Polytechnic is now a University, where coincidentally, I was to work many years later). I managed to pass the course and achieve the HNC qualification. This then took me to the final year of the Institute of Purchasing Supply course, which was run at Wednesbury College. The College was situated just off Junction nine of the M6, about ten miles from Birmingham City centre. Luckily around 1980, the M6 was nowhere as busy as it is today. Finally I achieved the purchasing qualification, which would help with my future career, and I was grateful to Roger for pushing me to do this.

In 1980, Alcan Plate were about to embark on a major project to introduce new plant to the factory. A new Annealing (softening) Furnace Line, Cranage and Construction work were part of the Project. At that time I was a Senior Buyer. I was asked to join the Project Team, with the title of 'Chief Purchasing Officer, Plant'. We were based in a Portacabin at the rear of the factory. Eric Walker would remain as Chief Purchasing Officer in the Buying office. He was due to retire in 1983, which would coincide with the end of the Project. I would then return to the Buying office and take over his role.

The Furnace Line we were buying was being supplied by a German company, Junkers. At the start of the process we spent a week negotiating terms and conditions with the German contingent. The Alcan Group Purchasing Officer was our main negotiator. The whole process provided great experience for myself. The Junker party had their interpreter along, who had his work cut out, when complicated conditions needed to be explained. Every so often a nodding and smile would break out from them, but sometimes a shake of the head would happen, then further discussions would take place before we could move on to the next point to be agreed. On the Friday afternoon, after five exhausting days, a deal was struck, with handshakes all round. More by luck than judgement, it had been agreed that payments would be made in Deutschmarks (this was prior to the Euro), rather than in pounds sterling. At the end of project we had saved about half a million pounds, on the original purchase price, due to the fact that the exchange rates had been in our favour.

The Furnace Line was coming from the German factory in sixteen sections, which would then be assembled at the Kitts Green factory. Each section was basically the same to form the Furnace Line, which would be about fifty yards long, they would be numbered one to sixteen. The individual units were coming by road, with the route being via Belgium. I am not sure how well this route had been scrutinised, because we had a message to say that section number one had hit a bridge in Belgium and had been damaged. Junkers decided to return this section to their factory for repairs and it was then be renumbered, as section sixteen. The other sections were then renumbered, and section two became section one, and so on. Needless to say another route was found, which did not include any low bridges. Apart from this the project went well and was completed pretty much on time, in 1983.

The project was high profile, and the company managed to arrange for Prince Phillip to officially open it. Unfortunately, the day Prince Phillip arrived, there was a technical problem with the Furnace, and it was not working. I recall him looking down the line into the furnace, expecting something to emerge, with senior management figures around him trying to make their excuses. After this initial embarrassing part of his visit the Duke of Edinburgh, was ushered to a room where a buffet had been prepared. Representatives of the workforce, including myself, had been invited to attend. Prince Philip moved around the room, and talked to us in groups, in the way that members of the Royal Family, seem able to do, in relaxed way.

CHAPTER 13

London Calls

The first London Marathon took place in 1981. Myself and a few other members of the Centurion Running Club, were keen to take part in 1982, some having completed local marathon/s the previous year. Those of us who had completed a marathon, would also be able to book a place at the start used by experienced runners. The other start would be used by the people who had not previously ran a marathon, which would be a much larger number, than the start we were using. In 1982 the entry was about sixteen thousand. In 2013 the numbers were approaching forty thousand. I recall that my training had gone well but did not seem to be as focussed as the training for my first Marathon, when the motivation was driven by the fact that it was my first Marathon, with the outcome being unknown. I travelled down to London on the Saturday, with Steve and a couple of other runners' club members. We had booked in to a Hotel close to Euston Railway Station, making it convenient for train travel down from Birmingham. We all shared a room, and the price that we paid reflected the standard of the Hotel. The wardrobe in our room was basically a curtain hung against the wall, which had a few coat hangers behind it. The beds were really all we required, so it fulfilled its purpose.

After we had booked into the Hotel we made our way to the Registration Point, which was close to Piccadilly Circus. There we were given our numbers, a bag to put our belongings in at the start, and other information about the race.

There was also going to be a Pasta Party there on the Saturday evening, which we decided not to attend due to distance from our Hotel. We found an eating place, not far from our hotel and looked to include plenty of carbohydrates in our meal. The next morning we shared a taxi to travel to the start. There were plenty of buses close to the start area, each having a number of the alphabet at the front, which related to runners' surnames. The buses were where you placed your bag containing your belongings, to be collected after the Marathon. I took off my tracksuit, and placed it in the bag, with one or two other items, put some Vaseline on important places, and was ready for the race. I took the bag and placed it inside the bus which had an 'F' on the front. I also had a spare black bag, with slots in it for my head and arms. I could put this over me to keep me warm till the race began. Once the gun had gone off, it was only a few seconds before I crossed the line, being at the experienced runners' start. At the other start, it may have taken a few minutes before a runner crossed the start, depending on where a person was in the mass before the start. Organisers usually have runners stand in the position that related to their expected finishing position, i.e. a person expecting to finish in about three hours, would stand in front of a runner expecting to finish in about three and a half hours. In more recent marathons, runners are able to use a sensing device which activates when they pass through the start, to give an accurate starting time, in order that their actual marathon time can be recorded.

My strategy for the run was no different from the one that I had employed for my previous marathons, take it easy for the first five miles, get into my running, and see how it goes. After a couple of miles the two pools of the race, the experienced runners and the first timers, merged together and the race incorporated its full numbers. At the six mile point, the *Cutty Sark*, the famous tea clipper ship, which was to suffer from an horrendous fire some years later, came into view. There were stewards standing in front of the concrete bollards, which were alongside the ship, then, to avoid runners having painful collisions. On then to cross the Thames over the historic Tower Bridge, around the halfway point, and then round by the Tower of London itself, with its stony pathways. I had not been aware of 'The Wall', a point where energy runs out, in my previous marathons, but I knew the eighteen mile point was generally regarded as the likely distance where it could happen. Whether it could be described as 'the wall', I am not sure but after eighteen miles, I seem to run out of energy, and started to walk. I had only stopped running for a few seconds, when I heard a voice from the side of the road, "You're not going to walk, are you?"

I looked over and there was a young girl, about ten, or eleven looking at me, with questioning eyes. I think I then sighed and started running again. The rest of the marathon was a struggle. I would jog from drink station to drink station, and have a little rest at each, whilst I drank or poured water over my head. In the early days of the London Marathon the finish was over Westminster Bridge, on the south side of the river. More recently the finish is in The Mall, running away from the Palace. In the original route, when I was running along the Mall, I was about three miles from the finish, running in the direction of Buckingham Palace. I was not feeling particularly good at that point, but half way down the Mall, I heard a few shouts, it was my sister and some friends, and as I turned they took a photograph of me. The photograph turned out well, and to my surprise I did not look as bad as I felt. I then continued onto Birdcage Walk, and eventually the welcome sight of Westminster Bridge, with Big Ben on the right, appeared in front of me. I went through the finish, with my time showing three hours twenty-one minutes, a little disappointing at the time. Someone put a medal around my neck, and an aluminium blanket around me to keep me warm. All I needed was something sweet. I passed through the finishing area and sat down with my back against a wall by a garden area, still not feeling great, and definitely requiring a sugar boost. I sat there for a few minutes. There was a lady sitting a few feet away, who was just opening a flask. I think she noticed I was not looking too good, and asked if I would like a drink of coffee.

"Does it have sugar in it ?" I asked.

She told me it did. I said, "Yes, please."

Within a few minutes of having this sweet drink, I felt much better, and was off to find bus 'F', to retrieve my tracksuit. I then made my way to meet Steve, and our other club mates at the pre-arranged meeting point. Steve was happy as he had ducked under three hours, but our other two companions had not fared as well, time wise. In hindsight the experience of the London Marathon was great, in terms of the spectators, the bands along the route, and everyone who was clapping and supporting the runners whether they were two hours ten minute elites, or the runners dressed in all sorts of outfits, who were going to take six or seven hours.

CHAPTER 14

Cardiff

The National Transplant Games in 1982, were being held in Cardiff that summer. This would also be used as a selection process to for the British Team who would compete in Athens, in the international games. After the London Marathon I concentrated my training on my events for the British Games in Cardiff, the 1,500 metres, and the five kilometres. I would incorporate track work into my training schedule. By now after initial advice from John Walker, I had worked out some training sessions myself, although from time to time, I did chat with John and he would give me suggestions of what to include. My training would still be mainly 400 metres repetitions, but sometimes I would include 200 metres, and 600 metres. The session would be something like four laps jogging as a warm up, then two 400m, followed by a 200m, 400m, 600m, 400m, 200m, and a couple of 400m to finish. The intention was for the 200m to help with speed, and 600m, to help with maintaining the pace I wanted to run at. One of the runners, from the club, asked if he could join me in a track session, one night. He thought it would help with his running. I said that was fine but warned him that I had been doing it for a few weeks, and he might find it difficult, on this first session. He was ex-navy with the tattoos to prove it. We had a few ex-military guys come to the running club, who liked to keep fit, after they had finished their service. All these guys were decent runners, who had had to maintain fitness during their time in the military. We went through a track session, basically, as described above, and at the end of it, I plonked down on the grass, trying to get my breath back. I looked up to see my naval training mate, jogging on the spot, enquiring what were we doing next. Times like this are useful to bring you down to earth, and make sure that you are not getting too big for your boots (or in my case running shoes). Ok, in the transplant world I was a good middle distance runner, but generally, I was no more than an average club runner, if that.

During the Games at Cardiff, the Transplant Olympic Association, of which I was a member of the management committee, held a general meeting which was open to all. We were looking to recruit some extra people on the committee and one of the items on the agenda was to ask for people, who would be interested to put their names forward. One person who did this was a gentlemen named Peter Griffin. Peter was the Transplant Surgeon from Cardiff Infirmary, who was the Chairman of the Cardiff Games. He was to become an important figure, within the Transplant Olympic movement, as he was keen to make it more democratic, in terms of there being elections for committee membership. Once Peter become established on the management committee, this happened and eventually members had to apply for re-election every three years. Peter was a hard working committee member for many years, although he did not always endear himself with some of the other members of the Committee. He was not always tactful and could at times rub people up the wrong way. He suffered from diabetes, which eventually meant that he had to give up surgery, so the transplant games became a very important part of his life.

My training had gone well, and I was hopeful of selection for the British team through my performances at Cardiff. On the Sunday morning I lined up for my five kilometre run. As previously, the start was on the track in the stadium, it would also finish there. One of the people lining up with me was Paul Silcox, who was a local lad from Cardiff. I knew Paul from the British team who participated in New York. The surprising thing was that Paul was a sprinter, and a very good one, so what was he doing lining up for the mini marathon. I had a quick word with him, and he said that he thought he would try and find another string to his bow, so he had been doing a bit of distance training. As the race started, keen to do well I went off in front, at a good pace. Paul soon joined me and we continued at a good pace but one that I was comfortable at. Paul stayed with me for about five hundred yards, at which point I felt he was struggling, and he started to fall back. I kept up a consistent pace and soon felt that I was well in front of the other runners. With about a mile to go I looked round and no one else was in sight. I was not going to slow down, I wanted to get a good time and hopefully make the international team. The ladies race had been run separately, but as I ran into the stadium, with a full lap to run, the leading lady was no far in front of me. I was focussed on finishing the race and I overtook her, about halfway round, and went on to finish. I found out later that it was her first transplant games, and she had done really well. I regretted that instead of overtaking her, I had not ran in with her and we had crossed the line together. In the afternoon I competed in the 1,500metres. I had a fairly comfortable ride, winning by a good margin. At the Gala Dinner in the evening, we were told that the British team for Athens would be announced, after the meal. I was with my Birmingham team and was the only one of us, at the table with expectations of being selected. At the point of the announcement, we were advised that twenty people had been selected, ten people in the 'A' team, and ten in the 'B' team. The team was read out by Peter Griffin, who had been appointed as the British Team Manager. Peter read out the names of the 'A' team, with no mention of myself. Then he read out the 'B' team, and I was relieved my name was included. I was pleased that I had made the team, but slightly disappointed not to be in the 'A' team, after my performances. Malcolm, who had been part of the selection committee, came and spoke to me afterwards. What had happened was that the selection committee wanted a strong sprint relay team, in the 'A' team, with four sprinters. Malcolm had argued that I should have been in the 'A' team, and thought that I would not weaken the relay team, to any degree. He was out voted and I ended up in the 'B' team. Basically, countries were allowed to send more than one team, but they were scored as individual teams. In terms of how it affected people in the British team, was that if you were in the 'A' team, you were paid for, if you were in the 'B' team, you needed to raise your own funds.

The 'A' Team was : David Davies – Sheffield

David Lindsay – Liverpool

David Lawrenson – Liverpool

George Heslop – Newcastle

Edmund Coady – Cambridge

Paul Silcox – Cardiff

Ruth Hudson – Manchester

Francis Hilton – Manchester

Valerie Disley – Manchester

Eileen Fitzharris – Liverpool

B Team: Peter Frazier – Birmingham

Simon Lee – Oxford

Ray Evans – Cardiff

Chris Wright – Guys

John Copley – Sheffield

Thomas Wright – Manchester

Angela Dunn – Cambridge

Maureen Bannister – Liverpool

Debby Lambourne – Manchester

Cindy Walters – Oxford

CHAPTER 15

Athens

Through various contributions, quiz nights and other fund raising activities, I managed to get the funds together for Athens. All the 'B' team managed to do this and where they had problems, or had a shortfall, the Management Committee were able to help out, enabling all the selected people to participate in Athens. My family were keen to support me, and my mom, dad and sister also decided to make the trip. Athens in August was going to be hot, and I was pleased to hear that my events would be in the evening, although surprisingly both on the same evening. We would be there a few days before the competition, which I was happy about, because I knew that I would need to acclimatise, as the atmosphere in Athens had a reputation for being poor.

We were transported from the airport on the evening of the arrival, by coach, and accompanied by a friendly and pleasant Greek gentlemen named George, who was to be our guide for our stay in Athens. We were to be housed in a medium sized hotel, called the Kristina, close to the centre of the city. I am not sure whether we were unlucky, and I would not suggest they were typical of the locals, but the staff at the hotel were not particularly responsive. It was typical to ask about three times before for you received any action, e.g. if you wanted a boiled egg for breakfast, it was best to ask the night before. I will put it down to the weather, it was very hot, and we would usually observe the local tradition of resting in our room, which I shared with my dad, in the afternoon.

On the morning after we arrived, I walked to the local park, with my dad, and jogged round for about half an hour, to help with my acclimatisation. It was warm but the atmosphere did not seem to affect me that much, which gave me confidence, that the local climate not going to be a major factor. There was still three or four days before competition to get used to the local conditions. The transplantation programme in Greece was struggling, at that time, hence the organiser's keenness, to bring the international games to Greece, to gain as much publicity from it as possible whist it was being held. A decision was taken, to change the name of the Transplant Olympic Association of Great Britain, by the management committee. The reason for this was that 'Olympic', has special significance, in Greece, which related to a certain event that takes place every four years, with its historic roots, on Mount Olympus. The new name agreed by the management committee, was the 'Transplant Sports Association of Great Britain'.

The local food, apart from that served up in group hotels, was not greatly enjoyed by our party. The traditional moussaka, was usually served up to suit the Greek palate, which is understandable, but it was not to the British taste, and quite greasy. If you ordered meat it seemed to be your luck as to which part of the animal you received. I, certainly for the most part, would order omelette and chips, when out and about, apart from the formal social events where the food was provided. I would not grumble about the wine Retsina, or Ouzo, but I have to say I did not indulge until after I had competed. After one glass of ouzo, I went to bed one evening, and as I lay down the room started spinning. I can only think I was a little dehydrated, but it was definitely strong stuff, and I cannot remember the size of the glass.

Athens was the venue of the first modern Olympics, in 1896, and the stadium we would be using for the athletic events of our Games, was the Stadium used for the 1896 Olympics. The stadium was called the Panathenaic. It was almost like you would see in an ancient chariot race, but in 1986 the capacity for the stadium was 80,000 people. The straights were long, with very tight bends, at each end. The stadium was open at one end, with a few steps leading up to the entrance. The recent marathons held in Athens, including the marathons in the last Olympics, held in Athens, finish in this stadium.

On the evening of the Opening Ceremony, we marched into the Panathenaic, and lined up in national teams in the central area, to listen to the speeches. After the Ceremony certain events would take place, on this evening, the first being the mini marathon (five kilometres), which I was competing in. At the end of the opening ceremony, Orien Young, our British team coach, grabbed me and said I needed to warm up. The start was at the rear of the Stadium. It seemed to be quite a long time before the start of the race. We were told by the race stewards, that we finished in the Stadium, and when we came into the Stadium we should get onto the track and run down the home straight to the finish line. They also said that a Police car would be in front of us, to show the route. I always made sure I listened and understood any instructions, given at the start. Just before the race was due to commence, Orien came over to me and exclaimed, "Gold for Great Britain!"

I took this as his motivational speech, or effort on his behalf to ensure I concentrated my mind on the task ahead. The Gun was fired and off we went. There was a short incline and then a turn to the right to along straight road. Right from the gun, at least seven or eight runners went off a fast pace. I was not going to be left behind, and kept with them. Gradually after the race settled down in the straight road runners began to fall back. It was not long before I found myself in front, and not aware anyone close behind me. I think I had run about a mile when the Police car in front of me, came to a halt at a main road, with its indicator signalling right. There was no way I was going to stop so I overtook it, turned right, and ran down the pavement of the main road. Soon the Police car was back in front of me on the main road. I recognised the road and knew that it took you to the front of the Stadium. There was about a quarter of a mile to go, I was running well, and feeling good, but I was aware of a runner close behind me. As we ran towards the steps at the entrance to the stadium my pursuer overtook me and ran into the stadium. Instead of staying on the track he ran across and appeared to make a bee line for the finish. I did as instructed and stayed on the track, and accelerated. The stewards shouted at my rival to get onto the track which he did, but he was then behind me and I ran the finishing straight to the finish line to win.

My fellow racer was Australian. His name was Michael Maladay, and ex lifeguard from Bondi Beach. He later asked me the question, how I was feeling when he overtook me, and whether I thought the race would have had a different outcome if he had stayed on the track. I was feeling good, and I certainly felt that I would have pushed to overtake him before the finish, but whether I would have done or not, we will never know. At the end of the day, the record shows that I won the race, and Michael was gracious enough to understand that, and settled for his silver medal. At the end of the race some children came up and asked for my autograph. Certainly a new experience for me but quite a pleasant one.

On the same evening the 1,500 metres took place on the track with its long straights and tight bends. I felt good and on a high after the five kilometre victory. The race progressed, and I was running comfortably, but for some reason was not up with the front guys. With about three quarters of a lap to go, I was aware of Orien shouting at me to close the gap with the leaders. This was the wakeup call I needed, and in the back straight, I made the effort to get to the two leaders, who were about twenty yards in front. I was running well and as I got up to them I overtook the two runners, at the head of the bend, and went in front. As we came into the long finishing straight, the black runner who was previously in the lead went passed me like an express train. I don't think I even made the effort to try and catch him, as before I knew it he was well ahead of me. I finished second well ahead of the next guy who would take the bronze. He was the runner from Holland who was third in the five kilometres in Central Park, two years earlier. We shook hands after he crossed the finishing line. The winner of the race was from the USA, he looked quite powerful, and I doubted if I could compete with him in a sprint. I was happy with my night's work, a gold and a silver, and I could relax having completed my events on the first night of the games. After these two races Peter Griffin came up to me, gave me a hug, and gave me his congratulations on winning the medals. His words were something like, 'well done, two golds would have been better, but a gold and a silver, is pretty good'. I think he was relieved more than happy, as the night up to that point, had not been going too well for the British team. When I got to bed that evening, my dad said to me that I had run two great races that night, and at that I turned over and slept with air of contentment.

Whilst our stay in Athens a one day cruise had been arranged from the port of Pireaus. The cruise took in three islands, and really gave a flavour of the non commercialised islands around Greece. It was beautiful day, with a cloudless sky and blue sea, it was idyllic. I particularly liked the relaxing atmosphere, on the seafront areas, of the small towns, with seating areas in front of the bars and cafes close to the sea where local fishing boats would rest in the calm water. I can't think of anywhere else that you could find which would be so relaxing if you wished to get away. Around this time Malcolm and Tony Barnes had discussed circulating some information to the medical profession, about how quickly people had returned to being active, after transplantation. They thought this would be useful information, where appropriate, for advising patients, post transplant, on their recovery programme. The publication was called *Physical Recreation After Renal Transplantation*, a copy of this publication is included in this book. Malcolm had circulated his survey to a number of international teams, and a number of British Competitors. It included such elements as medication; which was basically Azathioprine, and Prednisone, of various dosages, time after transplant that people resumed physical exercise, any specific injuries, and how many children were born to transplanted people. His paper was published in a medical magazine, and he gave me a copy of it. One sentence ended in the words, 'including one patient who ran three marathons, in just over three hours'. There had been some local publicity about my medal success in Athens. The story had appeared in the *Birmingham Evening Mail*. When I made my next visit to the running club, after returning from the International Games in Athens, I walked into the changing room, and the lads started to applaud. Not a lot was said, but I think it was a recognition that one of theirs had done well, and they showed their appreciation, which was very nice, and I allowed myself some satisfaction.

CHAPTER 16

Lands End To John O'Groats

John Walker and his friend Tom O'Reilly had decided to take on the Lands End to John O'Groats run at that time. I offered to be one of their support team. Tom was a two hour twenty marathon runner. They were looking to run seventy miles a day for the 850 mile route. We were travelling in two vehicles, large caravanettes, which had been donated, and also petrol had been provided by one of the large fuel companies. Some hotel accommodation, and shower facilities, were also sourced by John, in order that he and Tom would have a few nights, with a proper bed and bathroom. As part of the support team, I could be driving, helping out with the food, running a stretch with one of the runners, usually ten miles, and generally assisting as required.

The non-running project organiser, who came on the trip, was a friend of John and he had been a very good athlete in his time. He brought along his girlfriend, to help out. She told us the story of the early days of their relationship. He was booked in to run in the Boston Marathon, a run where you have to be an experienced marathon runner and have run under a certain time to be allowed to enter. He decided to enter her in the marathon, and lie about her not having run before, and give her an eligible time. She started running around the block, where she worked at lunch times, to get in some training. The day of the Boston Marathon, was very hot. After trying to get a good time, he had collapsed about two hours into the Marathon, and was taken to hospital. She had finished in a time of three hours and nine minutes. It seems she was a natural runner, and then proceeded to run several marathons afterwards. Her times were good enough that she even managed to get herself sponsored. The company who sponsored her was an egg producer, but she decided to drop them after a while, as 'Goldenlay', on the front of her running vest produced some embarrassing remarks.

During my days away on the Lands End to John O'Groats run, I took the opportunity to write my best man's speech for Steve Price's wedding, which was taking place a couple of weeks after my return. Steve had asked me to be his best man, a request that I reciprocated a couple of years later, for my wedding. Steve was marrying Denise, a fellow runner, who had been part of the jogging club for some years. She only lived about two hundred yards from the Sports Centre, and the jogging club, and the social side, had been a large part of her early life.

My best man's speech mainly related to when John Walker and members of the Centurion Club, had been invited down to the sea, for a weekend, by the 'Sailing for Disabled Children' charity, as a thank you for raising funds for them. We arrived there quite late on the Friday evening, in the pitch dark, only to find that our accommodation was on boats which were moored out in the bay. Our bags and cases were loaded onto a small boat, and using a bit of licence, I described the situation basically as follows, 'Steve volunteered Denise to lay prostrate over the bags so we did not lose any whilst we were rowed to find our designated boats in the bay, where we had been billeted for the weekend. Steve and I and couple of other guys had been allocated to a boat called the 'Loe'. Other people including Denise were to be housed in some other boats. Finding the boats in the bay, late at night in the pitch dark, had not been an easy task. On board the 'Loe', I found my bed to be basically a wooden board, where I placed my sleeping bag. My feet would slide into a cupboard, at one end, of the space limited cabin. I don't think the seamen were very tall in the century the boat was manufactured. Love blossomed over the weekend, between Steve and Denise', well that was the gist of my speech anyway. Although the weather was murky, the weekend was enjoyable, certainly a good two days on the 'Loe'. We had a boat trip round the bay, which was very pleasant, and we saw the 'Soren Larson', the ship used in the TV series the Onedin Line.

Back to the Lands End John O'Groats trip. We would get moving every morning about seven o'clock. John and Tom would set off with the two bike riders in front. The riders would have a map, to ensure they followed the correct route. The second caravanette would travel to the first stop off point, usually about ten miles ahead. Refreshments, or any other requirements, would be made ready so as soon as the runners arrived, they could be serviced quickly, and off on the next leg. The first few days went well and John and Tom were keeping to their target of around seventy miles a day. Then disaster struck, John managed to slip into a ditch and strained a muscle. He struggled to the end of the day and we managed to get hold of a local physiotherapist to attend to him, but the outlook was not good. John, however, insisted he was going to press on. It was decided that Tom should go on ahead, as John did not want to hold him up, so the team was split up, and I stayed in John's team. He continued bravely for the next two or three days, with the help of some physio, when it could be arranged, but he was well behind schedule, and had little choice but to give up. Tom and his team, had made it into Scotland, but he too, sustained an injury and had to call time on the venture.

It was an interesting few days, but I did not see John O'Groats, and up to this time that is still the case.

CHAPTER 17

1984

I984 was certainly, for me at least, not how George Orwell had predicted, well I don't recall any marathons in his book anyway. My fifth marathon was on the agenda for that year, the Wolverhampton Marathon, which had a reputation for being well organised. I completed the marathon, in about three and a half hours, although the final uphill finish was not pleasant. A few days after the marathon, I was in the changing room at the sports centre when One of my running mates came out with,

"I think you have got your shorts on the wrong way round!"

"No I haven't," was my response, checking to see what he was on about. Then after looking at the label, I agreed with his observation.

"Yeah, I think you're right," I said, " But you know what this means?"

"What?" he said.

"Well these were the running shorts I had on for the Wolverhampton Marathon," I answered, "No wonder I found it hard!"

After the marathon, I turned my attention towards the Transplant Games, which were returning to Portsmouth. The International Games were due to be held in Amsterdam that year and I was keen to be selected for the British team. For whatever reason my training had not gone that well, and my performances at Portsmouth reflected this. The following were the age categories at the Transplant Games; Adults – under 35, Senior – 35 to 44, Vet – 45 to 54, Super Vet over 55.

At 34, I was approaching the end of the adult category, and was up against some competitors who had started to emerge, that were a few years younger than myself. I was forth in the five kilometre, and third in the 1,500 metres, and was expecting the worst in terms of selection for Amsterdam. However, we were not restricted to the numbers, as in previous world games, and Malcolm, who was part of the selection committee, successfully argued that as I had brought back medals from the two previous internationals, and should be given my chance in the team on the back of this. There was about six weeks between the British Games, and the International Games in Amsterdam.

I would need to get some serious training in, if I was to attain a level to allow me to compete even with other British team members. I decided to consult John Walker to see what he would recommend. John proposed that I included, in my training, a session that he had done, when he was track running, in his younger days. It was basically designed for the 1,500 metres, but it would improve my speed generally. The session was to run ten one hundred metres continually. John told me that when he did it, he would have sprinters running alongside him. He would run the 100 metres, turn round at the end of the straight, and run the next 100 metres, and so on, to complete the ten sprints. I included this in my training, but would run it at about 90% of my full sprinting pace. For the next six weeks, I trained hard, and was pleased how it went.

We flew to Schiphol Airport, Amsterdam, and then to our hotel near the centre of Amsterdam. Malcolm had been appointed Team Manager, with Orien in his usual coaching role. A similar programme to that employed in Athens, was produced, in terms of the Mini Marathon being immediately after the Opening Ceremony, however the 1,500 metres, would be a couple of days later, and there would be heats. I would have British team mates in the Mini Marathon, these being John Murray, the young runner, who I had shared a room with in New York, and Pat Murphy. Both these guys had beaten me in the same event in Portsmouth. John had come to the fore recently, and his times were faster than mine, according to Orien. They both lived in the Portsmouth area, so Orien was helping John with his training. In the previous year, we had both ran in the 1,500 metres race. I knew that John had a faster time than me. I went to the front, as I usually did, and on the second lap John came up to my shoulder. I was expecting him to overtake me, but he didn't, and after a few seconds he fell back, and that's where he stayed as I went on to win the race, reasonably comfortably. He seemed to have some mental block about overtaking me at that time, although he was definitely faster. Once he had overcome this, he would go on to dominate the event in the next few years.

Once the Opening Ceremony was coming to a close, Orien told myself and the other British lads who were taking part in the Mini Marathon, to start to warm up for the event. We were told that the route was either marked out, or there would be stewards to direct us. The Opening Ceremony was in a large park area, which is where the race would start from, but the finish would be in a stadium. As in the previous international, I decided that I would keep up with the front runners at the start, no matter what pace they were going, unless there was a suicidal 'Australian' runner doing a Usain Bolt. As the gun went off I shot to the front, and then followed the directions which took us on to the road. Malcolm was standing a couple of hundred yards down the road, and as I passed he shouted, "Keep going Pete, you're going like a bomb." I hoped this did not mean I was going to blow up at any second. We were then directed off the road and into a country area. Shortly after that, I was aware of a runner whom was close to me. He quickly overtook me and was off. I recognised him, he was a Swedish runner who I knew was very good. I knew that if I tried to catch him up, I would definitely have 'blown up', so I continued at a good pace, but one that I was comfortable with.

The area we were running through was dominated by sports pitches, mainly soccer and hockey, there seemed to be hundreds of them. Then we came to a wooded area, I could not see anyone in front or behind, but I just kept following the path. I was getting slightly concerned because I was sure I must have run at least five kilometres, but there was no finish in sight. I still continued on

Police Class of 1969, at Ryton-On-Dunsmore. I am centre of middle row.

GB Team for Athens 1982 Athens.

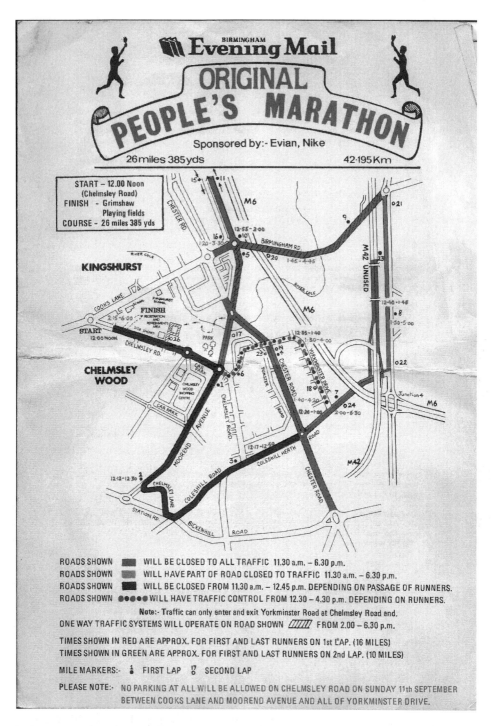

Peoples Marathon – Chelmsley Wood 1980.

London Marathon 1982.   Running down the Mall.

Medal Presentation 5k Athens. Left to right: Michael Maladay, myself, and Finnish runner.

Birmingham Volleyball Team. Back: L to R -Manjit, Eddie, Paul, me. Front: Tony, Kay, and Keith.

London Marathon Transplant Team 1990. Ian Wooldridge in Front holding Champagne.

On top of the world

By DEREK WEEKES

TAKING on the world — that's kidney transplant patient Peter Frazier, who scooped the awards in the British Transplant Games in Glasgow.

He did so well that he has been nominated for the national team in the World Games in Budapest from August 27-31.

Runner Peter, aged 41, a senior buyer for Birmingham City Council, won the senior men's victor ludorum in Glasgow, with gold medals for 5km and 1500m in the senior men's category, and a bronze in the 100m. The Birmingham team were runners up in volleyball.

Everything has gone well for Peter since his transplant in 1978 and he ran the London Marathon last year.

Peter, of Bartley Close, Olton, Solihull, who is the membership secretary of the transplant sports association of Great Britain, said: "There are only about half the number of transplants available that are needed and we hope events like this will raise people's awareness of the need for donors."

More than 4,000 people are awaiting kidney transplants, and 587 waiting for heart or heart/lung transplants.

Transplant swimmer Kay Simmonds, from Wolverhampton, will also be joining him in Budapest — she got three golds and two silvers.

Newspaper article 1991, after Glasgow Transplant Games.

A young 'Lucas' with Kasey.

Newspaper article after Sydney Games.

Transplant man scoops medals

SOLIHULL sportsman Peter Frazier has achieved more than he bargained for at the World Transplant Games in Sydney, scooping two medals.

Mr Frazier, 47, of Bourton Road, Olton, travelled to Sydney as part of the 81-strong British squad of transplant patients. He won a gold medal in the Mens 800 metres, and a silver medal in the Mens 1,500 metres.

Mr Frazier had a kidney transplant in 1978 at the Queen Elizabeth Hospital, Birmingham, after contracting a virus and spending six years on dialysis.

The life changing operation meant the Birmingham City Council worker could become increasingly involved in sport, and Mr Frazier has

By Louise Palfreyman

travelled around the world to compete in the transplant games.

Mr Frazier said: "I'm very pleased with my success as I had some problems in training and wasn't expecting to do so well.

"The games were very well organised with a superb opening ceremony and a parade past Sydney Opera House.

"In Australia, the organ donation rate isn't so good, so the publicity generated by the games will help."

More than 1,200 competitors from 53 countries came together to compete in a huge range of events.

All athletes have undergone heart, lung, kidney or liver transplants, and the British squad scooped nearly 50 medals, including 17 golds.

Mr Frazier was particularly moved by a new initiative at this year's games giving families who have lost relatives and consented to organ donation the chance to participate.

He added: "Representatives who lost relatives were involved in the games presenting medals, which must really help them.

"These days, transplant patients are encouraged to write to the family after a donation to say how appreciative they are.

"At the time of my transplant it wasn't done, but I think it would be nice if the family knew I've had a normal active life."

*After medal presentation for 800 metres, Vets – World Transplant Games Sydney 1997.
GB/USA/Spain.*

A thousand reasons why it's great to be alive

By PAUL SHEEHAN

Ceremony – World Transplant Opening Ceremony – Sydney. Opera House steps with teams from around the World -1997.

Competing in
Belfast Games 1998
'Not far to go, I
hope!'.

Congratulations – 25 years or more extra life!

[1] MACLEOD, N – ADDENBROOKE'S, LONDON – 04/11/1966 [2] BIRTALL, M – ROYAL LIVERPOOL – 01/07/1968 [3] BRADY, B – ADDENBROOKE'S, LONDON – 02/12/1968 [4] NIELSEN, V – ST GEORGE'S, LONDON – 16/09/1969 [5] FROUDE, M – ROYAL FREE, LONDON – 19/04/1970 [6] FORSTER, M – NORTHERN GENERAL, SHEFFIELD – 08/10/1970 [7] JONSON, V – CHARING CROSS HOSPITAL, LONDON – 03/11/1970 [8] ARNOTT, R – BELFAST CITY – 31/01/1971 [9] BUNDY, L – QUEEN ALEX, PORTSMOUTH – 27/02/1971 [10] BROCK, S – ADDENBROOKES, LONDON – 01/03/1971 [11] BRANDHAM, S – CHARING CROSS HOSPITAL, LONDON – 02/08/1971 [12] HARVEY, D – KING'S COLLEGE, LONDON – 26/12/1971 [13] FIEDLER, H – ST BART'S, LONDON – 19/01/1972 [14] MORRIS, W – ROYAL FREE, LONDON – 26/05/1972 [15] HARGREAVES, B – ST MARY'S, LONDON – 11/06/1972 [16] DOBBS, G – UHW, CARDIFF – 08/07/1972 [17] MASH, G – ST MARY'S, LONDON – 26/08/1972 [18] MARCHANT, B – GUY'S, LONDON – 22/09/1972 [19] KERR, A – BELFAST CITY – 20/02/1973 [20] RUSSELL, J – BELFAST CITY – 22/04/1973 [21] SIDAWAY, C – HEARTLANDS, BIRMINGHAM – 01/06/1973 [22] GRANT, J – BELFAST CITY – 23/10/1973 [23] ANGEL, A – UHW, CARDIFF – 03/11/1973 [24] BONE, J – MORRISTON HOSPITAL, SWANSEA – 07/11/1973 [25] JONES – ROYAL BOURNEMOUTH HOSPITAL – 28/11/1973 [26] HART, K – ST JAMES LEEDS – 13/12/1973 [27] PALMER, B – KING'S COLLEGE, LONDON – 01/01/1974 [28] KEAN, D – WESTERN INFIRMARY, GLASGOW – 11/06/1974 [29] EYLES, S – QUEEN ELIZABETH, BIRMINGHAM – 02/07/1974 [30] SHEPHERDSON – ST JAMES LEEDS – 04/07/1974 [31] ALLEN, J – GUY'S, LONDON – 30/07/1974 [32] STEVENSON, J – WESTERN INFIRMARY, GLASGOW – 14/08/1974 [33] EDWARDS, S – WREXHAM MAELOR HOSPITAL – 17/09/1974 [34] MARKHAM-LEE, M – LONDON HOSPITAL – 12/12/1974 [35] NEWEY, A – CHURCHILL, OXFORD – 31/01/1975 [36] CAWTHORNE, T – NORTHERN GENERAL, SHEFFIELD – 04/04/1975 [37] SKEHAL, L – WESTERN INFIRMARY, GLASGOW – 15/05/1975 [38] BRINN, A – ST BART'S, LONDON – 20/05/1975 [39] CLARE, H – ROYAL LIVERPOOL – 25/06/1975 [40] CHARLTON, L – FREEMAN HOSPITAL, NEWCASTLE – 26/06/1975 [41] MOXLEY, E – ROYAL LIVERPOOL – 12/07/1975 [42] SANSOM, P – ROYAL FREE, LONDON – 05/08/1975 [43] JESSUP, P – GUY'S, LONDON – 01/09/1975 [44] MOUNTFORD, M – NORTH STAFFS – 15/10/1975 [45] GREEN, J – GUY'S, LONDON – 12/11/1975 [46] JOHNSON, J – ST JAMES LEEDS – 10/12/1975 [47] PIGGOT, S – ST BART'S, LONDON – 23/12/1975 [48] MORRIS, S – WALSGRAVE, CONVENTRY – 01/02/1976 [49] LAWRENCE, J – ABERDEEN ROYAL INFIRMARY – 03/03/1976 [50] MORTON, A – BELFAST CITY – 09/03/1976 [51] HARRISON, I – ST JAMES LEEDS – 15/03/1976 [52] COX, A – CHURCHILL, OXFORD – 01/05/1976 [53] FORD, P – QUEEN ELIZABETH, BIRMINGHAM – 03/05/1976 [54] BILLINGTON, M – ROYAL LIVERPOOL – 13/05/1976 [55] ARMITAGE, D – CHURCHILL, OXFORD – 29/05/1976 [56] MOSLEY, J – CHURCHILL, OXFORD – 01/06/1976 [57] WILLIAMS, W – CHURCHILL, OXFORD – 31/07/1976 [58] PRITCHARD, T – GUY'S, LONDON – 12/08/1976 [59] BUNDY, N – GUY'S, LONDON – 19/08/1976 [60] HOLGATE, D – ROYAL FREE, LONDON – 17/09/1976 [61] THOMPSON, A – GUY'S, LONDON – 28/09/1976 [62] CARTER, M – ST BART'S, LONDON – 06/10/1976 [63] KEHOE, P – GUY'S, LONDON – 01/11/1976 [64] TOMSETT, B – ADDENBROOKES, LONDON – 04/11/1976 [65] GREEN, M – ROYAL FREE, LONDON – 08/11/1976 [66] CHAPMAN, J – NORTHERN GENERAL, SHEFFIELD – 07/12/1976 [67] HOLMES, B – ST BART'S, LONDON – 15/12/1976 [68] PULLEN, C – GUY'S, LONDON – 17/12/1976 [69] BLEEKER, J – PRESTON ROYAL INFIRMARY – 26/01/1977 [70] WILLIAMS, A – GLOUCESTERHSIRE ROYAL – 28/01/1977 [71] GRIMSHAW, P – MANCHESTER ROYAL INFIRMARY – 01/02/1977 [72] FARNHILL, L – UHW, CARDIFF – 02/02/1977 [73] HARRIS, D – ST MARY'S, LONDON – 02/02/1977 [74] FULTON, G – SOUTHEND GENERAL – 09/02/1977 [75] ANDREWS, A – BELFAST CITY – 19/02/1977 [76] GATES, B – ST MARY'S, LONDON – 01/03/1977 [77] JOHNSON, M – ADDENBROOKES, LONDON – 17/03/1977 [78] WARRIOR, L – LONDON HOSPITAL – 21/03/1977 [79] MATRUCCIO, N – CHURCHILL, OXFORD – 14/04/1977 [80] DONOHUE, T – ST MARY'S, LONDON – 22/04/1977 [81] MARTIN – ROYAL FREE, LONDON – 09/05/1977 [82] PHILLIPS, Y – ROYAL FREE, LONDON – 14/05/1977 [83] MAIN, R – ST JAMES LEEDS – 16/05/1977 [84] VENTHAM, L – ST BART'S, LONDON – 01/06/1977 [85] WATTS, A – WALSGRAVE, CONVENTRY – 28/06/1977 [86] WALLBANK, J – ROYAL FREE, LONDON – 01/07/1977 [87] LEWIS, D – QUEEN ELIZABETH, BIRMINGHAM – 07/08/1977 [88] FLINT, J – DERBY CITY HOSPITAL – 23/08/1977 [89] HERON, M – ROYAL INFIRMARY EDINBURGH – 23/08/1977 [90] HOOD, R – ROYAL DEVON & EXETER – 14/09/1977 [91] WOOFFITT, L – ROYAL LIVERPOOL – 15/09/1977 [92] ALEXOPOULOS, C – ROYAL DEVON & EXETER – 20/09/1977 [93] DAVIES, C – UHW, CARDIFF – 01/10/1977 [94] EMERY, J – NORTH STAFFS – 13/10/1977 [95] McCAW, A – WESTERN INFIRMARY, GLASGOW – 29/10/197 [96] FUNCHIEN, S – CHARING CROSS HOSPITAL, LONDON – 15/11/1977 [97] THATCHER, J – SOUTHMEAD HOSPITAL, BRISTOL – 10/12/1977 [98] WEBB, J – GUY'S, LONDON – 12/12/1977 [99] FOX, D – NORFOLK & NORWICH – 29/01/1978 [100] MALONEY, G – LONDON HOSPITAL – 13/02/1978 [101] MORGAN, J – ST JAMES LEEDS – 24/02/1978 [102] THOMPSON, M – ADDENBROOKES, LONDON – 25/03/1978 [103] DUNSTAN, D – MANCHESTER ROYAL INFIRMARY – 31/03/1978 [104] WILSON, R – CROSSHOUSE HOSPITAL, KILMARNOCK – 09/04/1978 [105] CLARKE, R – ST BART'S, LONDON – 10/04/1978 [106] PODMORE, J – NORTH STAFFS – 08/05/1978 [107] COOMBE, V – SOUTHMEAD HOSPITAL, BRISTOL – 07/06/1978 [108] MASKEY, R – BELFAST CITY – 26/06/1978 [109] DAVIES, J – MORRISTON HOSPITAL, SWANSEA – 05/07/1978 [110] SELLICK, S – LONDON HOSPITAL – 30/07/1978 [111] McKAY, R – ABERDEEN ROYAL INFIRMARY – 01/08/1978 [112] BODDINGTON, P – NORTHERN GENERAL, SHEFFIELD – 05/09/1978 [113] FRAZIER, P – HEARTLANDS, BIRMINGHAM – 08/09/1978 [114] FRANKLAND, A – GUY'S, LONDON – 09/09/1978 [115] BURGESS, M – ST BART'S, LONDON – 01/10/1978 [116] MARKHAM, T – WESTERN INFIRMARY, GLASGOW – 04/10/1978 [117] CROOKES, A – UHW, CARDIFF – 23/10/1978 [118] DAVIE, J – QUEEN ALEX, PORTSMOUTH – 16/11/1978 [119] HARDING, C – ST GEORGE'S, LONDON – 16/11/1978 [120] WOO, L – ST GEORGE'S, LONDON – 27/11/1978 [121] JOHNSTON, M – BELFAST CITY – 28/11/1978 [122] PHILLIPSON, C – ROYAL DEVON & EXETER – 30/11/1978 [123] ANDERSON, G – WESTERN INFIRMARY, GLASGOW – 01/12/1978 [124] PERKS, A – QUEEN ELIZABETH, BIRMINGHAM – 06/01/1979 [125] HEARNE, K – QUEEN ELIZABETH, BIRMINGHAM – 07/01/1979 [126] BROWN, H – ROYAL FREE, LONDON – 15/01/1979 [127] TIBBLES, F – GUY'S, LONDON – 16/01/1979 [128] REEVE, D – ST GEORGE'S, LONDON – 22/01/1979 [129] LOWTHER, J – ROYAL LIVERPOOL – 11/02/1979 [130] BISHOP, S – SOUTHMEAD HOSPITAL, BRISTOL – 12/02/1979 [131] FURBER, V – MANCHESTER ROYAL INFIRMARY – 13/02/1979 [132] HARRINGTON, M – GUY'S, LONDON – 14/02/1979 [133] SHANE, J – ST MARY'S, LONDON – 01/03/1979 [134] MAYELL, J – GREAT WESTERN, SWINDON – 04/03/1979 [135] JENKINS, A – QUEEN ALEX, PORTSMOUTH – 16/03/1979 [136] LAWRENSON, D – NORTHERN GENERAL, SHEFFIELD – 26/03/1079 [137] HARTLEY, J – ST JAMES LEEDS – 08/05/1979 [138] KEETCH, C – UHW, CARDIFF – 19/05/1979 [139] HODSON, L – FREEMAN HOSPITAL, NEWCASTLE – 30/05/1979 [140] LINES, A – GUY'S, LONDON – 31/05/1979 [141] ROPER, J – GUY'S, LONDON – 01/06/1979 [142] KEYWORTH, C – CHURCHILL, OXFORD – 02/06/1979 [143] WARGENT, L – HEARTLANDS, BIRMINGHAM – 17/06/1979 [144] ORMAN, O – NORTHERN GENERAL, SHEFFIELD – 20/06/1979 [145] JENKINS, G – LONDON HOSPITAL – 16/07/1979 [146] GOSLING, P – ST MARY'S, LONDON – 01/08/1979 [147] FROST, R – ADDENBROOKES, LONDON – 05/08/1979 [148] DAYKIN, J – MANCHESTER ROYAL INFIRMARY – 01/09/1979 [149] PHILLIPS, S – MORRISTON HOSPITAL, SWANSEA – 01/09/1979 [150] GHAFFAR, Z – LONDON HOSPITAL – 01/10/1979 [151] EYRES, T – ADDENBROOKES, LONDON – 17/10/1979 [152] BARCIO, D – KENT & CANTERBURY HOSPITAL – 10/11/1979 [153] COOPER, T – LONDON HOSPITAL – 19/11/1979 [154] STEELE, B – WALSGRAVE, CONVENTRY – 23/11/1979 [155] CRANE, D – MANCHESTER ROYAL INFIRMARY – 02/12/1979 [156] SCAPLEHORN, P – UHW, CARDIFF – 05/12/1979 [157] GANT, C – ADDENBROOKES, LONDON – 22/02/1980 [158] McKAY, H – ABERDEEN ROYAL INFIRMARY – 04/04/1980 [159] HORNER, B – SOUTHMEAD HOSPITAL, BRISTOL – 01/05/1980 [160] BRADLEY, G – NORTHERN GENERAL, SHEFFIELD – 03/06/1980 [161] CORPS, C – ST JAMES LEEDS – 27/06/1980 [162] LIDDLE, L – NORTHERN GENERAL, SHEFFIELD – 19/08/1980 [163] HALL, C – QUEEN ALEX, PORTSMOUTH – 24/09/1980 [164] ATTRIDGE, P – QUEEN ALEX, PORTSMOUTH – 19/06/1981

List of kidney recipients with over 25 years success rate. (circa.2006)

Olympic Torch Relay- Leamington Spa Parade 1st July 2012.

Carrying the Olympic Torch −2012.

After the Torch Relay with L to R: Jack, Lucas, me, and Jonathan.

My wife and I.

Physical Recreation After Renal Transplantation

M. H. Simms and A. D. Barnes

SUCCESSFUL renal transplantation can restore patients with end stage renal failure to normal life, so that doctors looking after transplantees should expect to be asked about the advisability of physical exercise. The Transplant Olympic Games were launched in Portsmouth, England in 1978 by a transplant surgeon, Maurice Slapak, principally to increase public awareness of the value of organ donation. Despite the reservations of many doctors these competitions proved immensely popular and have had no harmful consequences, so that regular national championships and a biennial international championship are now organized under the aegis of a governing body.[1] In order to identify any special characteristics of transplant athletes we sent out a questionnaire to competitors in the 1980 Transplant Olympics in New York and the British Transplant Games in Birmingham (1980).

Replies were received from 54 members of five national teams (from Canada, France, Greece, Switzerland, and the United Kingdom) and 21 British regional competitors. These 75 patients comprised 57 men and 28 women aged from 12–50 years, mean 28.6 years. (In the United Kingdom the mean age of patients at the time of transplantation is rather older than this, mean 36 years[2].) Fifty (67%) were maintained by a first cadaveric graft, 21 (28%) by a first related donor graft, and only 4 (5%) by a second cadaveric graft. (In the United Kingdom 16% of grafts are from living related donors and 13% of cadaveric transplants are second or subsequent

From the Queen Elizabeth Hospital, Birmingham, England.

Reprint requests should be addressed to M. H. Simms, M.D., Queen Elizabeth Hospital, Birmingham, England.

grafts.[2]) Seven patients have never undergone dialysis and the remainder have been dialysed for periods between 3 months and 7 years, mean 1.8 years. Time since transplant varied from 3 months to 11 years, mean 4.1 years. Most patients were taking conventional maintenance immunosuppression with a mean Prednisone dose of 10.5 mg/day and of Azathioprine 110 mg/day. Twelve patients took alternate day prednisone and the recipients of related donor grafts took none but this did not seem to confer any obvious competitive advantage. Prior to transplantation half of the patients had been treated for hypertension and a third were on antihypertensive drugs at the time of the games. One-third of patients had had their own kidneys removed but this was not correlated with the continuance of antihypertensive drug therapy. Only six patients had suffered from metabolic bone disease and this did not restrict their choice of event at the time of the games.

Forty-two patients practised a sport regularly before developing renal failure, two at national level, and 55 had recommenced from between 2 weeks to 9 years (mean 16.6 months) after transplantation. The remainder were motivated to recommence by the stimulus of the games. The most successful competitors had resumed sport within a mean interval of 4 months from transplantation. Racquet sports (tennis, squash, badminton, and table tennis), running (at all distances) swimming and golf were the most popular activities but hockey, soccer, cycling, dancing, skiing, gymnastics, weight lifting, shooting, and even hang-gliding were all represented. Many transplantees compete regularly in open sport events and claim to have reached levels of performance they had never previously aspired to, including one runner who has completed three full marathons this year, each in just over 3 hours. Twelve patients had suffered a sport-related injury since trans-

Written by Malcolm Simms and Tony Barnes. My marathons get a mention.

plantation, all of which were nonpermanent and limited to the lower limb, including muscle strains, knee strains, and toe fractures. Only one woman and five men were not either fully employed, studying or running a home. Eight men had fathered at least 13 children since transplantation and two women had given birth.

All participants in the Transplant Olympics are amateurs and clearly posses a degree of confidence in their physical ability. The majority have avoided the worst morbidity of dialysis and transplantation and are maintained in good health by a first kidney graft after a moderate period of dialysis. Provided the patient's graft function is stable on maintenance immunosuppression, hypertension is controlled, and there is no active bone disease, there seems to be no reason to dissuade transplantees of any age from resuming sporting activities as they wish. They should be encouraged to undertake regular training before entering competitions. There is no evidence to prohibit any particular activity but we are aware that contact sports may be hazardous to the kidney in the iliac fossa and patients should be warned to seek medical advice before any new sport is commenced.

REFERENCES

1. The Transplant Olympic Association of Great Britain, U.K. Reg. Charity No. 280432

2. U.K. Transplant Service Report 1978–79, Bristol, U.K., U.K.T.S., 1979

but I was sure that I had run well over the distance. From nowhere, a runner appeared in front of me. I did not understand where he had come from. I was confused, but I thought at least I knew I had not got lost, and was on the right route and if nothing changed I was in the medals. After a few hundred yards a stadium appeared in front of me. As we got closer, the runner in front stopped, and directed me into the stadium. I now understood, he was just someone who was ensuring runners took the right route. I ran into the stadium and onto the track. With a couple of hundred yards to go, I looked round, no one behind me, I clenched my fist, a silver medal in the bag.

As I stood at the finish, runners were coming into the Stadium. In fourth place was Pat Murphy. He fell over the line and virtually collapsed. Pat, as I previously mentioned, was a courageous runner, and had no doubt given his all, as was his character, but sadly he did not have a medal to show for it. John Murray was fifth, and obviously very disappointed with his performance.

With regard to the 1,500 metres, I knew my rival would be a fellow Brit, Martin Bexley, a young lad from London who had been in athletics prior to his renal failure, and the Swedish guy who had won the mini marathon by a distance. Martin was always accompanied by his dad. One thing about the Amsterdam Games, they were good at circulating times and results. Martin had not run in the mini marathon, but he and I were looking at the positions and times for the race, which had been pinned up in our hotel. Martin's dad piped up and proclaimed that Martin would have beaten my time, if he had run. I pointed out that I believed the race was much longer than five kilometres, more like seven kilometres, I calculated by my time, but I don't think his dad was convinced.

There were heats for the 1,500 metres, but, although I did try to find out, no one seemed to know what the criteria was for qualifying for the final. When I ran my heat, I treated it as a normal race, I went to the front and kept a good pace going. On the last lap, Martin Bexley, who was near the side of the track shouted to me, to slow down, as I was well ahead. I acknowledged him but continued at the same pace, not taking any chances about qualification, for the final. When the qualifying list came out, I was top with the fastest time, but I knew it would be a different story, in the final. The pace in the final was as hot as I had ever experienced in a race of transplant runners. On the third lap, there were five or six of us in the leading group running really hard. On the last lap the Swedish guy made his move and Martin chased him. I was running as hard as I could but the two front runners were out on their own. There was a gap behind me and I settled for third place. The Swedish runner was a good way in front of Martin, at the line. I was happy with my silver and bronze medals, especially after my poor performances in Portsmouth.

CHAPTER 18

Outside Of The Main Games

In 1982, I had suggested to the Transplant Sports Association of Great Britain management committee, that it would be good to have a competition outside of the summer games, which would be something else to offer to the membership.

My suggestion was that we had a competition, which would involve teams from the various British units, in a team sport. I came up with five-a-side football. Generally there was support from the committee, for my suggestion. However there was some concern about the sport being five-a-side football, as some committee member felt that there was too much physical contact in that sport. I was not a great expert on five-a-side football, but from the information, I had, it was supposed to be non-contact, and with reservations, I got the go ahead to organise the event.

I thought that the competition could be held on a Saturday. Birmingham being a central location, would be a good place to hold a weekend event, in respect of travelling for all the teams. I would arrange hotel accommodation for Friday and Saturday nights, in the centre of Birmingham. My thinking was that people would either travel to the hotel on Friday night, or go straight to event on Saturday morning, and then travel home on the Sunday. I needed to find a central venue for the event. The most suitable sports venue I could find was the Aston Villa Leisure Centre, a few hundred yards from Villa Park. Obviously this went against the grain, with my allegiance to their second city rivals, but for the right cause, one has to compromise, that's what I told myself anyway. I went to talk to the people at the Leisure Centre and was able to book a suitable Saturday, in April 1983. They also showed me a function room upstairs, where they could provide an evening dinner after the event. Through the local referees association, I managed to book some referees to officiate on the day. As part of the objectives of the Transplant Games movement was to gain publicity, for organ donation, my next action was for this element.

I drew up a 'Press Release', and circulated through the media sources. Liver and Heart transplants were becoming more common at that time. We had an entry of a heart transplant team from Papworth which the *News of the World* newspaper were interested in doing an article on. However the doctor from Papworth, would not sign the medical form of one of the heart tranplantees. He travelled to the event, but was not allowed to take part. The Papworth team did participate, although they had to borrow a goalkeeper. The *News of the World* did not run the story, as they wanted a full team of five heart transplants. We did achieve some good local publicity including local radio, and I was interviewed live during the afternoon. It happened that Aston Villa had a home match that day, and as I was looking to find someone to present the trophy, I thought I may be able to get one of their players for this task, and present medals to the winners and runners up. I wrote to the club, in this respect and had a reply from the then Aston Villa Manager, Tony Barton, who said he would be happy to come along after their game and present the trophy. Tony Barton was the manager of the club when they won the European Cup, in 1982.

The day went well and seems to be enjoyed by everyone. There were a few incidents which did suggest five-a-side football could not be described as a non-contact sport, but no serious injuries. We had a Birmingham team, of which I was part. Unfortunately we did not progress from the first round games, but it's not about winning it's the taking part, as I always said when not winning! We did have a good goalkeeper, a great lad from Shrewsbury, named Chris Evans, who was diving about all over the place. The winning team were from Newcastle, wearing the appropriate black and white stripes, of their famous team. Tony Barton arrived right on time about five thirty, to present the medals and trophy. He seemed like a really nice guy, who was happy to talk to the people after he had presented the trophy. Sadly Tony died at an early age, a few years later.

As we made our way up the stairs for the evening meal, one of the Newcastle lads, said to me in a strong Geordie accent, "It's been a canny day." Not being Geordie speaking myself, although my great grandfather was born in Newcastle, I interpreted this as, 'Its been good day', I think! The evening and food were fine, but once the meal was over, people were getting a bit restless, until the coaches arrived to take them back to the hotel. I made a mental note of this and decided that if I arranged similar future events, the evening dinner should be at the hotel. People like to go back and change after they have competed, and after the meal they can do their own thing, or we could have a disco that could go on till late at the hotel.

When I reported back to the Management Committee, everyone thought that it was a good idea to hold an event such as this away from the main games, but the sport should not be five-a-side. After discussion Volleyball was the favoured sport, and it was one that we had started to include in the summer games, plus it was definitely non-contact. I was happy to organise a volleyball competition the following year, in November, with a similar format, apart from the location of the Dinner, which was going to be at the hotel.

CHAPTER 19

1985

1985 was the year I got hitched, and pleased to say I am still happily married to this day. I married Gill Ford on the 19 October 1985, and also inherited two step-children Theron and Nicola. Gill had been widowed the year before. Her first husband John, as previously mentioned was chairman of the East Birmingham Hospital Kidney Patients Association. John was a nice guy, who cared about the welfare of fellow kidney patients. John was very sporty in his younger days, prior to his health problems, which caused his renal failure, and subsequent dialysis. He was always playing football or cricket, and was creating a promising career at Land Rover, when his health problems forced him to give up work, at quite a young age. John had several problems, related to very high blood pressure, where his balance was badly affected, through damage to one of his ears. In fact his doctors could not understand how he was able to walk unaided, knowing the damage to his inner ear. About two years before he died he received a kidney transplant, which did give him some respite from dialysis, but the years of high blood pressure, and other problems had done their damage. John did in fact take part in one Transplant Games, where he held his own playing table tennis, which he very much enjoyed. He was always very supportive of my Games involvement, so it was good that he was able to participate, even for one Games.

More about my marriage later in this chapter, but onto my sixth marathon.

Whether in the British Games or the International Games, the people from Northern Ireland that I met where always the most friendly and chatty. People like Joe Raffo, and his wife, and both Janet Greaves and Janet Coleman (regular internationals), were always up for the crack, as they called it. When they advised that the main beneficiary of the Belfast Marathon, in 1985, was the Northern Ireland Kidney Research Fund, and asked me if I would run it, and maybe bring some other transplant marathon runners with me, how could I refuse. Being Belfast in 1985, I did have some reservations, especially when told that part of the course was along the Falls Road, which had a bit of a reputation related to the troubles. I was in touch with some of the transplant runners I knew had run marathons, and was able to get a commitment from John Murray, and a Scottish lad, David. I wrote a letter to my contact in Belfast, to confirm there would be three of us taking part in the marathon. I posted this letter at 3pm in the afternoon. The following morning, about 9am, the phone rang at work, and when I picked it up, the first words, I heard in an Irish accent, were, "Its great that three of you are coming."

"How do you know?" I replied.

"Well it's in your letter."

I could not believe the letter had got there so quickly. If I had sent it to another address in Birmingham, I bet it would have taken 48 hours.

The Northern Ireland Kidney Research Fund was a substantial charity. Part of the money they raised was used to fund the wages of staff at Queens University, carrying out research into kidney disease. They arranged our flight tickets and accommodation in Belfast. There are two airports for Belfast, one in the city itself, and the other is about ten miles out of the city. We arrived at the latter, and were collected at the airport. On our journey into Belfast we passed some army vehicles, and soldiers with rifles, who were patrolling around estates on the outskirts of the city, and I wondered if my decision to come was sensible. We were driven to the 'Forum' Hotel, where we would be staying. The frontage was fenced with barbed wire on top. They advised that the 'Forum' was the most bombed hotel, in Belfast, which again did not help with my feeling of, 'What have I let myself in for?' Joe Raffo was one of the Belfast party, who were looking after us during our stay. Joe was a transplant patient, who had run the Belfast Marathon previously. He had some health problems, and was not feeling too good at that time. He had undergone operations on his stomach, and told us that he would not be running in the marathon, although it was his original intention. Joe owned a Fish and Chip Shop in Belfast, which was run by himself, and his sons. He took us to his home, where his wife prepared a lovely meal, finished off with homemade raspberry pavlova. We were showed round Belfast and at every bar we were shown, I hasten to say that we did not have a drink in every bar, the comment from our hosts was, 'Alex Higgins was banned from this Bar'.

On the night before the Marathon, we were invited to a reception, put on by Guinness, who were the major sponsor. We were given a record, *The Belfast Marathon*, and a Guinness tie. During the evening a few of us were interviewed by the local radio. I am not sure what I said but next morning I woke up to my dulcet tones, talking about marathon running on the radio. My training for the marathon had been disrupted by an Achilles tendon problem. The tendon, which is at the back of the lower leg, about ankle height, swells, and the only cure is to stop running until it returns to normal. This would take about a week, and then I needed to resume training, gradually, starting with short runs on soft surfaces, mainly cross country and having to ice the ankle, before and after running. The icing would usually be done by way of a bag of frozen peas, from the freezer, for ten minutes each side of the run. I only got eight weeks of continuous training prior to the marathon, but I had a plan and would keep to running at a pace that would allow me to finish the twenty-six miles and three hundred and eighty-five yards, I hoped. My comfortable running pace for a long distance, with the restricted training I had been doing was about eight minute miles, which would give me a projected time of three and a half hours for the marathon. I also knew that with my the background of disrupted training I was likely that the last few miles would be a struggle. I therefore expected my time to be around three thirty-five/three forty, which I would be happy with. The other element that had become clear, which I am not sure related to my kidney related health background, or drugs, was that I needed to have a sweetness intake. This had been happening at the end of races, but I figured it would help if I introduced this earlier. I decided to take some glucose tablets with me and regularly take them during the marathon run.

The marathon route was fine with many areas of the city, being very pleasant and no different to those that you would find in many other large cities, in the UK. I was running well in the early stages, and sticking to my plan of eight minute miles and regularly having a glucose tablet. In the later stages, as I expected, things got harder but I struggled on and managed to finish in three hours and thirty-six minutes. My predicted time was pretty much right, which gave me a good sense of achievement and I thought that considering the problems I had running up to the event this was probably the most satisfying marathon I had run. John and David had come in a few minutes prior to myself. The marathon control was advised and a little later an announcement was made to the crowd that all three transplant marathon runners had successfully completed the course. Another transplant runner finished in four hours something, but it did not matter about his time, it was Joe Raffo. With all the problems he had generally, and specifically in training for this marathon, and his insistence that he would not be running, he ducked under the radar and did it again.

Joe was to go and win a gold medal, at an international games, in the future, in a swimming race. What a great bloke! During our stay at the 'Forum' hotel, there had been a television programme being filmed there on the first floor. The first floor being where the main bar area was. One day I came down on the lift, and in error had pressed the first floor button, instead of the ground floor. When the door opened, I could see they were in the middle of filming a scene, with the actors posed, and the bright lights shining. I quickly pressed the lift button, for the ground floor, hoping that no one had noticed my intrusion on the proceedings. Due to the filming, the main bar, on the first floor was sometimes closed. This was the situation later one day when the other lads and myself felt like a drink. The only other place in the hotel to get a drink was the basement bar, which was a gay bar. We decided to make our way down, tried not to make eye contact, and I subconsciously spoke in a high voice when ordering our three drinks. The morning after the Marathon, we were sitting in the hotel reception, in our track suits waiting to be collected, when a priest, who looked of high office, spotted us and came over, "Did you run the marathon yesterday?" he asked.

"Yes," we replied.

"Are you knackered?", which brought the same response.

Whist we were in Belfast we also had a look round some of the sporting facilities of the City, including the Mary Peters track. Dame Mary Peters is a national treasure in Northern Ireland, having done so much to encourage sporting activity, there, after her Olympic gold medal, in the Pentathlon, in 1972, many years before Denise Lewis and Jessica Ennis, achieved their success, in the event with two more disciplines, the Heptathlon. We were told by Irish friends how much she had done and how much she is admired in Belfast. She was actually in the Forum Hotel restaurant, having a meal, with some other people was one the days we were there.

After my return from Belfast my courtship of my future wife Gill, who had been widowed the previous year, moved forward. Having known each other for many years, related to the Kidney Patients Association, activities, I had asked her if she would like to go out, and she agreed. The relationship went well and we decided to get married later that year. We were married at St Margaret's Church, Olton, Solihull, at 2.15pm on 19 October 1985. The time of 2.15pm was not intentional, the service was originally due to be 1.30pm, but there had been a blunder at the Vicarage. A friend of my future wife, who attended church regularly, asked Gill about the date we were getting married. When Gill told her she said, "Well, that's funny, there was no record in the church diary."

We contacted, Mr Dodds, who would be conducting the ceremony, who confirmed that he had failed to record our wedding in the diary. He was most apologetic, and said he had never neglected to do this in his twenty years of conducting marriages. On that day he had a wedding at 1.30pm, and one at 3pm, but he would fit us in, between these times at 2.15pm. This suited me as at least I knew that it would not be too long a service.

Both Gill's children Theron and Nicola, were teenagers, who I had known for some years, and it was very pleasing to me that they were both supportive of my marriage to their mother. I am pleased to say after many years their attitude has never changed, and they continue to be happy that their mother and I got married. After the marriage service we went to the Bank House in Knowle, Solihull, for our Reception. The Bank House in Knowle, consisted of a large room, with wooden panels, which was partitioned down the middle. When we arrived there, everyone was initially in one side of the partition, for drinks, until called into the other side for the sit down meal. Steve Price was my best man, as I had been at his wedding. His speech included a reference to me being known as the 'white tornado', down at the running club, not because of my speed, but because I liked to throw talcum powder over myself in the changing room. After the Reception we spent our first night at the Metropole Hotel, at the NEC (National Exhibition Centre), which had a policy of offering favourable prices for special occasions, such as weddings, as we also found a few years later when Nicola had her wedding reception there. The following morning we travelled up to York for a few days on honeymoon. We stayed at the Station Hotel, which used to be the railway station, itself. On our first walk, we came across the Yorvik Centre, where there was a Viking Exhibition, York being a Viking settlement. The exhibition, which was basically a journey through Viking settlement, on the site of renovations in York, was very popular, and a queue, all round the square, and was past the sign that said, 'one hour and half wait'. We decided to come back earlier on another day. Which we did, a couple of days later, when the queue was a bit shorter. However, we had queued for about an hour, just as we got to the door, a school party arrived and they were allowed straight in, so we waited for another half hour. When we eventually got in, we boarded a movable car, travelling round the reconstructed settlement, for about twenty minutes, taking in the earthy smells, whilst listening to a recorded commentary from Magnus Magnusson ('I've started so I'll finish' – which he did).

On the Wednesday morning, the day before we were due to leave, I got up and looked out the window, and was surprised to see loads of policemen, and sniffer dogs, searching the gardens, at the back of the Hotel. When we got into the lift, to go down to breakfast, there was another couple also going down. I said to them, there was something going on here. They were surprised we did not know that Princess Ann was coming that morning to name a train. After breakfast we went for a walk, and when we returned, it was obvious that Princess Ann had arrived as there were security guys everywhere. The first floor of the hotel was being renovated, with all the rooms being empty and gutted. I wondered if we walked along the hallway on this floor, we might get a view of the train naming ceremony. As we got to the end of this hallway and looked down through the window, there was Prince Ann, no more than fifteen yards away from us doing her bit. We stayed there for a few minutes watching the proceedings, and then made our way back passed the derelict rooms, and through the door at the end of the hall. As we went through the door, there were four security men, standing at the top of the stairs with their walky talkies. When they saw us appear from this area, they seemed taken aback as we walked swiftly passed them, smiling to ourselves.

In November, of 1984, the first of Volleyball competitions, away from the main games took place, at the Aston Villa Leisure Centre, with the accommodation and Dinner and Disco, at a city centre hotel. I had drawn up the rules, and had them approved by the management committee, which was very much based on the general rules for volleyball. Six people in each team, with a team required to have a minimum of one girl, on court at all times. I did not want to have time-outs, because I wanted to run the games on a time basis, in order that events could be run on time. If we had two courts, as we did at the Aston Villa Leisure Centre, by the sound of the hooter both games could be started and ended at the same time. For some reason Volleyball had been a recurring sport throughout my life. It was a game we regularly played at school. When I was a new recruit, at the Police training Centre, at Righton-on-Dunsmore, volleyball was one of the main sports activities. In fact my Sergeant, made a comment on his report on me, that I was good at volleyball. I think he was struggling to find any other positive comment to make.

CHAPTER 20

My Early Life

I was born on the tenth of May, 1950, it was a Wednesday. They say that Wednesday's child is full of woe, but that definitely has not been the case with me, although, there have been one or two miserable days. I was born at home, in York Road, Hall Green, Birmingham. At one end of York Road, on the other side, was 'The York' Public House, with its white rose, as the pub sign. Across the road, at the other end, was Hall Green Dog Track. This was my maternal grandparent's house, where we lived till I was one. I was the second child of Irene and Stan Frazier. Sandra, my sister, had been born three years earlier. My parents were married in 1945, on the fourth of July, hard to forget. My dad was in uniform, on his wedding day, having been in the Air Force. His roll in the War was to drive lorries, carrying various supplies to and around the Air Force camps, and did at one point drive a Fire Engine at an Air Force base. In civilian life his profession had been as a polisher working in motorcycle manufacturers. He mainly worked at the Velocette Motorcycle Company, where his father Joe, also worked. My dad's first name is also Joseph, but he has always been known by his second name Stan. (Joe Frazier was a name made famous by a future boxing legend – no relation). He was a hard worker and would move around to other companies, if there was a shortage of work, but the Velocette would always have him back. My mother worked in the machine shop of the Velocette, in her younger days, and this is where she met my dad, before he went off to do his military service.

In 1951, a council house was allocated to us, in Thurlstone Road, Longbridge, Birmingham, and the Fraziers had a home of their own. Our house was on the top of a hill, which was very useful when we had our first car, a Standard, which my Dad tells me had a thirst for oil. A starting handle was sometimes necessary to start the car in those days. It was inserted in the front of the car, and turned by hand until hopefully the engine roared. If it did not then the next option was to push it. Fortunately, living at the top of the hill, meant that with a small push to get it moving to the downhill bit, usually it would start as it gained momentum on the way down. Mom and Dad had purchased a television set before we moved to Longbridge, and it moved with us. It was floor standing set made by 'Bush' and had a nine inch screen, increased to twelve inches by the magnifying glass, anchored over the screen. All programmes were black and white, with only the BBC channel available at that time. When I got home from infants school, at four o'clock, I had to wait an hour before watching the regular children's programmes, *Rag, Tag and Bobtail*, and the *Wooden Tops* amongst others. My sister and I would play out with the other kids from the road, or were always in other people's houses, playing with our friends. Hardly any traffic then, so games like 'kick the can', in the road were regular activities.

As well as working in the day time my dad also had a part time job, as a barman, at a pub called the 'Shaftmoor', in Hall Green, and also 'The York', across the way from my grandparents' house. My grandad Ernie, also did a bit behind the bar, at 'The York', but he only had to walk across the road. In those days all the barman wore white coats, behind the bar, and there were specific pub rooms; the lounge, the bar, the smoke room, and some even had a 'Gents Only'. It was pretty much of a ritual that on Saturday nights that we would ride over to 'The York', from Longbridge, to visit my mom's parents, Edith and Ernie. The adults would be in the pub, whilst my sister and I would be stocked up with pop and crisps, outside, in the grounds of the pub. Sometimes we would be with Ray, our mom's younger brother, who was six years older than me (a young uncle) and some of his friends.

My mom and dad decided they would like to run their own pub, at this time. My dad having done his training behind the bar, felt he wanted to give the pub trade a go. They applied to Mitchells and Butlers, one of the main midland breweries, at that time. I was seven, and just started junior school, when the offer came of a Public House, in Rugby, Warwickshire, called 'The Engine'. Leaving Longbridge behind, and some friends that we had made during our six year spell there, we were off to Rugby, about thirty-five miles from Longbridge. 'The Engine' Public House was three stories high, on the corner of a residential area of Rugby, about a mile from the centre. The address was Bridget Street, a working class district of the town. The Pub was probably built in the early part of the century. On the top floor there were six empty bedrooms, on the first floor there was an impressive room for a society called the 'Buffs', a bit like the 'Freemasons', but not so secretive. We also had a yard where there were a few tables and chairs for customers, and a swing. Outside of pub hours, the gates at the entrance to the yard could be closed for privacy.

When we first went there my mom and dad, could only find a Catholic School for me, which I went to for a week. The school was run by nuns, we had small blackboards and chalk to write with and combined with a full catholic service on the Thursday, I was all at sea, luckily Mom and Dad quickly discovered there was an junior school, near the town centre in Chapel Street. I was 'educated' there for the next three years. I did struggle for a while, although I was not that bright to start with, but Warwickshire Schools did things differently than Birmingham Schools. In my school in Longbridge, we were taught to use small writing. In my new school it was different, and large was the order of the day. I had not been at Chapel Street long, when in the English Class (undoubtedly my worst subject), we were given a sheet of paper with a series of parallel lines on it, and told to write about ourselves on the page. Apparently this was for some submission to some Education body. Possibly the nineteen fifties equivalent of SATS. I proceeded to write in my usual small script and handed it in to the teacher. Once she saw it, she immediately torn it up and threw it in the bin, with some scathing comment, about it being no good, and could not be submitted. It turned out that the writing had to fill the parallel lines, which seemed to me to be about a half inch wide, so my small writing was lost. The only subjects I was good at were Maths and Art. Although I was not in the top group generally, whenever we did a maths test, I usually finished ahead of my fellow classmates.

The school was usually short of teachers, in fact at one point, we only had two teachers, with two student teachers helping out. Teachers therefore took several subjects. The Art lesson was taken by an ageing tutor, who we liked very much, mainly because he would give you an apple if you produced a good drawing, and also because he was always making derogatory remarks about the Headmaster who he obviously did not have much time for. There was a time where everything I produced, art wise, was put on the wall. All the teachers would comment on how good my figures were, and would even stand over me whilst I was creating. Unfortunately, as relatively good as I was at art and maths, the opposite was the case with my reading and spelling, which to say was below par, is definitely an understatement.

The sports activity at school, was infrequent, and apart from the odd visit to the local park, amounted to football in the playground, where I was one of the better players, and usually the person who brought the ball. There would be an annual regional sports day and after having some age related qualifying races in our playground, myself and some others would go off to represent the school, in the various events, mine being the 100 metres sprint. I never got through to the finals, but I always enjoyed competing. One of my mates, who was a decent sprinter, came second in his heat. He told me his dad had said to him after the race, probably thinking he was onto a good thing, that he would buy him some running shoes if he came first in the final. My school friend promptly won the race and claimed his prize. It is amazing what motivation can do, just that incentive to give it your all.

The three years living in Rugby were generally pretty good. My mom and dad got on well with the locals, and seem to be regarded in a good light by 'The

Engine', regulars and staff. My sister and I also enjoyed our stay there, and have fond memories of Rugby. There were lots of places to go in walking distance, including the town centre. We had a local swimming pool and picture house. Most Saturdays with my pocket money of two shillings and sixpence (twelve a half pence in new money), I would be off to Woolworths, to buy an 'Airfix' kit, which I would make back at home. Usually there was more glue on my fingers than on the plastic plane, and my painting was decidedly dodgy, but the transfers were ok. The pub itself, because of its number of rooms, was a good place for hide and seek, and many other activities.

My dad had made a success of managing the pub, and obviously Mitchells and Butlers, felt that he could take on a new challenge. In 1960 when I was ten, we moved to the Marston Green Tavern, located in Marston Green, a village just outside Birmingham, on the south-east side. The Tavern was a very old pub, but the Brewery had planned to knock it down and replace it with a new pub. The old Tavern had been there for countless years. We had pictures of horses being tethered outside, it was probably an old coaching house, where travellers would stop for refreshments in bygone days. It was a great place in the summer with a large field at the rear, with tables and chairs for customers, and plenty of room for kids to play. There was also a wooden function room on the side of the field, just at the rear of the pub, which was called the 'Chalet'. On the other side of the pub, fenced off from the field, was a bowling green. It was a shame when the new pub was built in 1961, that the field, bowling green, and chalet, all disappeared to make way for a paved seating area, and a huge tarmacked car park.

Education wise I was still of junior school age, when we moved to the Tavern, and for six months I attended Marston Green Junior School. After assessing my ability, my teacher, a very astute and affable man named Mr Cooper, asked the question, "Are you sure you want to take your eleven plus ?"

I am not quite sure why I replied, "Yes", but it was probably my ego playing tricks. The inevitable happened and I was off to a secondary modern school, with the name of Kingshurst High School for Boys, for my senior education.

This school was just over three miles away, requiring the local authority to put on a coach to take the kids from Marston Green to Kingshurst, boys and girls schools. At the rear of our pub and Marston Green Village itself, there was nothing but woodland, until our school playing fields appeared after a couple of miles as the crow flies. A few year later the thousands of houses appeared in the form of Chelmsley Wood, and Marston Green would no longer be an isolated village.

I soon settled at my new school, and it helped that I knew some of my fellow pupils, from Marston Green Juniors, who like me, had failed to make it to a Grammar School. I did however make it to the top stream, and the fact that I had settled schooling for the next five year ensured that I did not leave education as a total dunce. My teacher, Mr Cooper, at Junior school, having quickly picked up that I was not academically bright, also soon gleaned that I was not bad at sports. Every Friday afternoon the class would go to the local playing fields, where Mr Cooper would select the two teams to play each other. It was always the same, Philip, Steven, and myself would always be on the same side, and would always be the forwards. Every week we would trash the weak opposition, and usually take it in turns to score the goals. I am not sure why he did this. I can only assume we would be the nucleus of the school team should we ever play another school, which we never did. The rest of the kids must have suffered from very low morale, and maybe would of benefited from more forward thinking motivational techniques. When it came to football at my senior school, whether it was the extra competition, or the fact that I did not develop the skills needed, I never seem to excel. Although I was considered for the school team on a couple of occasions, I never actually made it, to represent the school. We were a footballing school, as opposed to a rugby school. We were once challenged to a rugby match, by a local rugby playing school. I ended up in the team, and in practise with myself being on the wing, I touched down to score a great try, after an excellent move. In the interests of honesty, I have to say there was no opposition during our practise. When it came to the match itself, we were thrashed twenty something to nil, and no further rugby games were sought. My best subjects were still Maths and Art, and as an offshoot of these, Technical Drawing. Amongst other classes that we did in senior school were Woodwork and Metalwork. For the last two years at school, we had to do one or the other. I ended up in the metalwork group but I preferred woodwork.

One of my fellow pupils, in the woodwork group, who could be quite disruptive at times, had a bit of a spat with the woodwork teacher, to the point that they both agreed that a separation, was necessary. We were asked by the metalwork teacher, if anyone would like to move to the woodwork group, so this lad could join the metalwork. I immediately volunteered, and ended up in woodwork for the next two years. I enjoyed woodwork, well I liked wood and became quite good at it. At this point, I should mention that my wife, with some justification, is not complimentary about my handyman skills, although I was the first pupil in the school to successfully complete a hidden lap dovetail joint.

When I left school at sixteen, I had three GCE 'O' levels, in Maths, Art, and Technical Drawing. With three CSEs, in General Science, Woodwork, and English (Grade 4). My intention was always to join the Police Force. It was something that I always wanted to do, and also I had aspirations of having a successful career in the force, as my dad's younger brother, John, was making for himself, at that time. John reached the rank of Detective Superintendent, before he retired. He was well liked and highly regarded in the Force. I made efforts to join the Police Cadets, at sixteen, but at that time I was measured five foot six and half inches. If you were close to five foot eight, they did have some leeway, but I was a little too short at that time, and I was advised to come back when I was nineteen, and hopefully I would be tall enough to apply for the Force itself. I decided to find a job for the next couple of years, without any long team strategy, apart from as a stop gap, before I joined the Police.

About this time my parents had decided to come out of the Pub trade, after about nine years. We had moved to Steyning Road, in South Yardley, Birmingham. Dad had found himself a job as a machinist, at Land Rover, Clay Lane, which was just around the corner. My first job was at Beresford Pumps, as Production Control Clerk. It was a time when you could walk into a company, and ask if they had any jobs, with the likelihood of a positive response. When I walked into Beresford Pumps, and asked the question, the answer was yes, we have two jobs, which one do you fancy? Ok start on Monday. I worked at Beresford Pumps for about seven months. I liked the factory environment, and the people there generally, but the guy I worked for, who had been described as woolly by the personnel manager, was a strange character. He seemed to have a high opinion of himself, although I could not figure out why. Fred was getting on a bit, and spent most of his time sitting at his desk, smoking his pipe. When he wanted something done he would usually ask me to tell someone to do something. I was not happy with the situation so I started to look around for another job. I found this at W. Canning, in Hockley, a well known company, and at one time a world leader in electroplating where I was offered a job as office junior, with a view to move on to be a junior estimator. I gave in my notice and moved to W. Canning, in March 1967. I stayed at this company for two years, the last twelve months as a junior estimator, until I joined the Police Force.

CHAPTER 21

My Police Days

In May 1969, at the age of nineteen, I started my training, with Birmingham City Police Force. For the first two weeks, my fellow recruits and I attended Tally Ho Police Centre, in Edgbaston, close to the Cricket Ground, for initial briefings on our future career. One of the first things that happened, was the issuing of our Police uniform, and instructions of how to wear it. We were still in the days of separate collars, epaulettes needed to go onto shirt collars, and a truncheon in the pocket. The entire kit was given to us, which was quite heavy and bulky. Those of us who were not driving at that time, like myself, struggled to the bus stop, to get ourselves home, with the uniform in toe. During this two weeks, at Tally Ho, we were taken round the various police divisions, in the city. 'A' division was the city centre, with the main Police Station being Steelhouse Lane (now opposite the main entrance of the Childrens' Hospital). 'B' Division was around the Selly Oak area, and the south-west side of the city. I most remembered 'C' division, because I thought, I did not want to be allocated to work in that division. As most divisions, 'C' Division had two sub-divisions. One that covered districts, including Handsworth, Hockley, and Winson Green (the home of Birmingham Prison). The main station, in this division, was Thornhill Road, Handsworth. The other sub-division was Ladywood, and surrounding area. The main population of Handsworth and around was West India and Asian, two communities who did not, for the most part, get on particularly well.

After the first two weeks we were off to the regional Police Training Centre, at Ryton-on-Dunsmore, for the next thirteen weeks. Here we would come into contact with recruits from other midland forces, such as Leicestershire, Coventry and Warwick, and West Mercia. We were allowed to come home for weekends, and I managed to get a lift, from a fellow recruit, Ted, in his van, as he passed close to my house, in Yardley. Everything was provided at Ryton, which was based on army basic training camp, apart from the classroom work, which was mainly concerned with ensuring that we had a workable knowledge of the criminal law. We did have individual rooms, which were in what could be described as army huts, with food provided in a communal hall. We had regular drill training, from our army trained sergeants, geared to the passing out parade at the end of the course. The hairdressers would attend every two weeks, and you were in trouble if you had not attended, or had not pressed you uniform, to the required standard. Our class was made of about eighteen recruits. Every four weeks we would have a written exams to assess our understanding of the law we had been taught, up to that point. My results after the first four weeks, put me about midway in the class. After the second exam, even our sergeant, expressed his surprise, when he read out the results, and I was second. I put this down to me getting my head round how the law works, in particular the 'Offences Against The Person Act', i.e. Section 1 – murder, section 18 – wounding, and section 20 – assault. Unfortunately, my third exam, went the other way, and my average, for the whole course, put me about midway for the class.

I had generally enjoyed my training at Ryton, but when they announced, at the end of the course, who would be stationed where the shine was initially taken away. We were all advised together our respective postings. When it came to myself and two other officers, the message was 'C' division, Thornhill Road. I would be working from Thornhill Road, Handsworth, and living in Single Men's Quarters, at Holyhead Road Police station. This was a small station manned by one officer, which had six upstairs bedrooms, where single men such as myself, lodged. Holyhead Road was a continuation of the Soho Road, which was the main shopping area for the West Indian and Asian community. Downstairs, at the station, we had a lounge and kitchen, where we spent most of the time, whilst off duty, when we not enjoying our social life. Much of the time when I was off duty, I would be playing cards with other officers who were in the station at the time. Social life would either be in the pub opposite, 'The New Inns', or visiting city centre clubs. The shifts would be nights on the trot (which I enjoyed, because there usually plenty going on, until about 2, or 3am), mornings 6am to 2pm (which I was not keen on mainly due to lollipop stand in), and 2pm to 10pm, which were ok. I made some arrests, mainly for being drunk and disorderly, and there were a few interesting incidents. It seems to me that it is human nature to want to go and look, if something is happening in your area. As a policeman you have the opportunity to do this, albeit, that you know you will have to deal with whatever confronts you. For me as a policeman it created a certain excitement, when you were travelling to an incident, and depending what information you had, it also created some trepidation about what you may encounter when you got there. I had not passed my driving test in the early days, in the force, so I spent most of my time on foot, or as a passenger, with a colleague driving. One day I was a passenger in a panda car, in a line of traffic, at a business shopping area, when a young boy was knocked off his bike by a car just a few vehicles in front of us. The boy was carried into a shop, and I got out of the panda, and rushed into the shop, to find him sitting on a chair. The side of his mouth was enormous, and I feared he had a broken jaw. When I ask him if he was ok, he said he was fine, and produced a large gobstopper from his mouth. On another occasion an alarm had gone off, in a secured office, at All Saints Hospital. We sped in the panda to the main entrance where a guy directed us to the room in question. As we ran in we came across a workman sitting on the safe painting the wall.

I was out in the Panda, with a colleague, one evening, in the Handsworth district, when we had a message over the radio to go to a local address, to respond to a 999 call. Off we went, at speed, to the location given, but no detail as such, as to what the emergency was. My colleague, was PC Bates, a popular member of the team, and known generally as 'The Master'. Neither of us were what you would call well built and both around 5'8", just.

When we arrived in the road, we observed an elderly Asian gentlemen waving furiously at us. We pulled up, and he pointed into to the doorway of his house and exclaimed, "He's breaking my house, stop him, stop him!" When we calmed him down and got him to tell us exactly what was happening, it seemed that he had had a disagreement with one of his tenants, who was about to leave but before he went he was intent on breaking up all the furniture. We got the landlord to show us which room he was in. I tried the door and it was locked but I could hear the most almighty banging going on in the room. I knocked loudly on the door and shouted, "Police, open the door". I heard a mumbling, but the banging continued. After a few more requests by myself and PC Bates, to get this person to open the door, we heard a click and it opened. In front of us stood a huge West Indian man, about 6'5" tall, wearing a tee shirt, with stretched sleeves, confirming his bulging biceps, which 'Arnie', would have been proud of. He was holding a sledge hammer. As both of us looked up at him, he shouted, "What you want?" Not wanting to escalate the situation, and fearing for both my, and 'The Master's', lives, I said to him, in a calm voice, "Can you stop breaking the furniture and leave the house".

"I ain't leaving anything for him," pointing at the Asian, landlord, cowering by his front door.

"This is my stuff, I'm breaking." We checked with the landlord and he confirmed that the furniture he was smashing, belonged to his estranged lodger. "OK", I said, "but you still need to be out of here." He turned went back into the room and after a couple of further bangs, he confirmed that all his stuff was destroyed, and he was ready to go. As he pushed his way passed the landlord, I was hoping he was not going to turn and say, in a slightly German accent; "I'll be back."

On another occasion a dog had been found and brought into Thornhill Road

Police Station. I say a dog this was a mountain of a dog, a gentle but huge Great Dane. In those days dogs would be kept overnight, and if not claimed, would be collected by the dogs' home the following morning. We were instructed, myself and a colleague, to take the animal, over in the Panda Car to Dudley Road Police Station, in the early hours, as there was no place to house it at Thornhill Road Police Station. It must have been a strange sight, if anyone had spotted this noble dog sitting in the back of the Panda, doing his 'Scooby Doo' impression, as we drove through Winson Green towards Dudley Road. As we walked into Dudley Road Station. PC Jinks who was in temporary charge of the Station, overnight looked at the dog, and then at us and in a mischievous way enquired if he had been for a walk.

"I don't want to take him downstairs till he has had a walk".

"OK, I'll take him", said my fellow officer.

It was about four in the morning when what appeared to be the latest, and certainly largest recruit, to the police dog section, was being exercised along the Dudley Road. When my colleague returned, after his stroll with the Great Dane, along the Dudley Road, he reported that all had gone well but a bus had nearly hit the pavement, as it passed them.

I did receive a commendation during my relatively short spell in the Police Force. This came about through the following circumstances. It was after midnight, and I was on my own patrolling the Soho Road in Handsworth. Over my radio came a message from the city's central control room, saying that an alarm was going off at a shop on the Soho Road, the name of the Shop was 'Nelson House'. When I looked at the shops, the one I was right outside was 'Nelson House', it was a tailors. There was a side entry on one side, I had a quick look down, but could not see anyone. Then I got on the radio to Thornhill Road. My number was C109, so the call was, "109 to Charlie 1", which would get me through to the Station Sergeant. When he acknowledged, I said, "I'm outside this shop with the alarm going off, sarge".

"Ok", he said, "just stay there, and we will send some assistance".

I then went down the side entry, and checked round the back, but again, I did not see anyone. Then I returned to the front and waited for assistance. A panda pulled up and Mick Jones, PC C99, stepped out. Mick said the key holder had been contacted, and would be there in due course to open up. We kept an eye on the back and side of the premises, and as I was there when the alarm went off, either the alarm had gone off by accident, or there could be intruders inside the shop. When the key holder arrived and opened up, Mick and I went into the shop to look round. Nothing on the ground floor, nothing upstairs. We did notice that there was a hole in the ceiling in one of the upstairs rooms. The key holder did not know if there had been a hole in the ceiling before. Mick and I were not satisfied, until we had checked this out. The key holder said he had a ladder in his van, if we needed it. We took up his offer and without delay the ladder was carried upstairs and placed against the hole. Mick climbed the ladder and shone his torch, around the loft area. He came down, and said that he thought something had moved, but he was not sure. At that time the dog handler had arrived, and brought the dog upstairs. If there was someone there we made sure they were aware we had a large police dog, with us. Mick then shouted up, "Either you come down or the Police dog comes up".

At that point we heard movement, and a figure appeared at the top of the ladder, and started to come down. Then a second man did the same. They kept well way from the police dog. Mick arrested one, and I arrested the other. A few weeks later, one of the force circulations advised that Mick and myself had been given commendations for these arrests. It turned out that these individuals had owned up to a number burglaries on the Soho Road, and this had solved quite a few outstanding crimes for the CID section.

CHAPTER 22

Other Activities

In 1984–5–6, I organised successful Volleyball Competitions, in Birmingham, away from the main Transplant Games. In 1986, I decided that, as with the main games, it would be good for different Units, around the country, to organise the Volleyball Competition each year, so we advertised, through our Newsletters. Other Units did come along, and the Volleyball still goes ahead, under a similar format to the original ones. Later through a similar initiative, Badminton was also added to the annual calendar of events. It was also around this time, that Malcolm Simms decided to resign from the Management Committee. Malcolm, and his wife Helen, had a young family, and with this and his surgical career he felt that he could not commit the time to remain. I totally understood this but at the same time, Malcolm was a loss to the management committee, not only for his abilities, but also because he was one of the most genuine people I knew and I would miss his involvement and support. Although, still a trusty of the Transplant Games Committee, Tony Barnes, also took a back seat, with regard to the day-to-day business of the Transplant Sports Association. His view was that it would over time be mainly run by the patients themselves, and the doctors would gradually take a back seat.

Maurice Slapak was still Chairman, at that time, but again he was happy for the day-to-day business, to be handled by the elected members who were up for election every three years. Maurice was a very good diplomat, who could always smooth the waters, should there be any conflict, which could happen from time to time, especially when international interests would surface. Maurice was very keen on playing and watching tennis. We had some of our meetings at the Queen's club in London, as he was friendly with the manager there. Should Wimbledon clash with the dates of the Transplant Games, we knew where Maurice would decide to make for, however, he could always gave his full attention to Transplant Games matters, either side of Wimbledon. I continued my role as membership secretary, we now had pretty much full membership of the association. We usually had about three management committee meetings, per year. One would be at the Transplant Games itself, usually on a Sunday morning, which sometimes would be a problem for me, due to the clash with the mini marathon. Because of my central location, we would hold committee meetings at my house, quite regularly, where my wife would be complemented, on the spread which she put on. She would also keep transplant surgeon, Chris Evan's daughter, Ruth, amused, during meetings, when she brought her with her.

I continued to compete every year, in my main events, and as part of the Volleyball team, but my results were not good enough to make the international team. I was getting older, and my running activities had diminished. I was not putting the effort in training so I could not expect to make the international team. My interest also moved for a while into dogs, and dog showing. Gill had always had cats. In fact when she moved house in 1985, she had three cats, but only one would move and the phase 'nobody owns a cat' seemed to be apt. Only one cat was actually persuaded to make the journey, of about hundred yards, and across the road. Of the other two, one was very old, but both were seen regularly having found themselves new feeders. In the late eighties, there had been a series of break ins, in the area. I have never been a great fan of burglar alarms, but I do like dogs, so I suggested to Gill, not expecting a positive response, that we should consider having a dog. To my surprise, she said ok as long as it was a breed that was good with children, maybe a Lassie collie. Gill had child minded for some years. When John was ill and at home, it made sense for her to find some work which would allow her to stay at home, and child minding fitted the bill. I was happy to go for a Lassie Collie, although I did not know a lot about the breed at that time, apart from they did have a reputation for being good with kids. My step-daughter Nicola, was a little miffed, stating, she has asked for a dog for years, without any success, and I had suggested it once and got the ok.

We acquired a sable rough collie puppy bitch, who we called 'Shelley'. 'Rough' Collies are known as Lassie collies, obviously due to the popularity of 'Lassie' in the films. The original Lassie in the film, was actually a male, as they preferred to have a larger dog to play the part. Shelley was a nice dog, and when she was two, I decided, I would like to have some puppies from her. It happened that she was not able to have puppies, but whilst looking for a male stud dog, we met some people who breed and showed collies, who became our friends. Chris and Mac Shutt, lived in Bilston, near Wolverhampton. We had a bitch puppy from them, she was a blue merle colour. Her name was 'Misty', originally Missy, because she had too much black colouring to be a show dog. We eventually had three puppies, from her. One of which, we kept, a blue merle dog named 'Kasey', who I wanted to show. Training was essential when 'Kasey', was young, and we would regularly take him to 'ring class', where he did very well. Many of our weekends were spent at Dog Shows, which could be mean travelling quite a distance, especially in the case of Championship shows. Kasey did qualify for Crufts, after winning a class, at a Championship Show. The judge happened to be the owner of Kasey's father (a champion stud dog), however when we spoke to him afterwards, he said he did not know that Kasey had been sired by his dog. I did get to show Kasey at Crufts. He was not placed in the class, but I was pleased that he looked good and performed well. Kasey showing career was cut short, as he developed some problem with his colouring, which we were not able to solve. After that we did not pursue showing dogs.

It was interesting, that a friend of Chris and Mac Shutt, had done some research on the history of rough collies. What he had discovered was that the breed was a result of interbreeding between the Russian Borzoi and the original sheepdogs from England, the type you would see in old paintings of the English countryside. This came about through the contact that the British Royal family, and the Russian Family had probably in the nineteenth century. Rough collies are certainly not the most energetic of dogs, and certainly not as intelligent as border collies, but if the dogs I had were a good example of the breed, they are lovely dogs to have.

I was in a pub one evening with a friend, Brian Cole, and a couple of Brian's mates. Gill and Brian's wife, Mo were off at some social event together. Brian had worked with Gill's first husband John, at Land Rover, and had been friends with him, since they were in their teens. Brian and Mo, were very supportive, through John's illness, and the family friendship continued when I married Gill. During our evening at the pub, the conversation came round to marathon running. One of Brian's friends, Brian Galloway, who I only met a couple of times before, and who just started to get into running, asked me what times, I had done. When I told him, he said, "You're almost an athlete." Years later when I was looking for a title for my book, this phase seemed appropriate!

CHAPTER 23

A Phone Call

In 1988, I had left my employment at Alcan Plate, after deciding I needed a change. I was now a 'Senior Buyer', in the Supplies Department at Birmingham City Council, earning a higher salary than the one I was receiving at Alcan, carrying the title of 'Chief Purchasing Officer'. I was never much for titles. I was soon to find out about the complications of public procurement, especially with European legislation shortly to be introduced. The City Supplies Organisation, of Birmingham City Council, was based in Nechells, a couple of miles from the City Centre. It had offices and a large narrow isled stores area, where supplies would be delivered out, via our own transport, to Schools, Social Services establishments and Leisure Centres, amongst other council premises. When I joined City Supplies the organisation had only been at these premises for two weeks. It had previously been owned by a fastening (nuts and bolts) company, who found that the stores set up, was not suitable for their business. Their customers would come to collect their nuts and bolts, but it was taking a long time to serve them, the reason being that most customers had a number of items they required. If they only wanted one item, the narrow isle system was fine but, the manually operated lifts necessary, meant that to pick a number of low value fasteners, from various isles, made the system uneconomical. Racks on one level, where the storemen can just walk up and down to pick items are much more suitable for collection of nuts and bolts and the like.

It was a Wednesday afternoon, in March 1990, I was sitting at my desk, in the City Supplies Office, when the phone rang. It was a lady who advised she had a group of transplant runners, who were running in the London Marathon, and knowing my background, wanted to know if I would be interested in joining them. I basically said she must be joking, as it was five and half weeks before the marathon, and I had been doing very little running at that time. She was very keen on me joining them, and I said I would think it over and let her know the next day. For whatever reason, I rang her the next day and said I would. It turned out that the story of a group of transplant runners was being covered by the *Daily Mail* Newspaper, and before I knew it, I was down in London, with the group of my fellow transplant participants. We had lunch at the Houses of Parliament, with a parliamentary gentlemen named James Wellbeloved, and the chief sports writer for the *Daily Mail*, at that time, Ian Wooldridge, who sadly is no longer with us.

In his first article, about the venture, Ian described myself as a veteran of six marathons, as the other participants had either not run a marathon before or had run two or three. I did know some of the people from the Transplant Games. Andrew Dibsdale who was one of the other runners, I knew, but had not regarded him as I runner. He told me that he had been training for this for twelve months. One of the girls, Bridget had been attending the games for many years, but again I only associated her with racket sports. Dee, a more recent participant, in the Games, lived in London. She suggested we all went to her house, on the Saturday night before the Marathon, for a Pasta meal, which we all agreed to. My training had mainly consisted of running round a local park in Olton, Solihull, where I now lived, with my wife, Gill. I decided to run on grass as much as possible, my thinking being that if I tried to build up too quickly, on hard surfaces, the likelihood of injury was increased. The fact that I had five and a half weeks to improve my running fitness, was concerning, but hopefully would be enough to get me round the course in whatever time?. Onthe morning of the marathon, I boarded one of the trains to take me to the mass start area. Extra

129

trains had been laid on, but even so I don't think I have been on a train with so many people. I could hardly move, and remember thinking, that if this trained crashed it would be the biggest disaster in the history of British Rail. Just before the start, I put my tracksuit and one or two things in the bag that had been provided, and placed on the double Decker bus, that had an 'F', on the front. Then I covered myself with a black bin liner, to keep warm until the start. It took about ten minutes after the hooter, before I passed the start.

My strategy was slightly different from previous marathons, in that I would start slow, and probably get slower, but although I was considerably slower than previous marathons, for obvious reasons, I felt ok for the most part. I got to the end of the Marathon, it had been a bit of a struggle, and for the last few miles, it had been a combination of walking and jogging. My time was about four hours, fifteen minutes. I was feeling reasonably good, certainly better than I had felt after some previous marathons, but I did feel somewhat tired. When, I met up with Gill, who had come down to collect me, with Nicola, and her husband Paul, I asked if she would go and retrieve my tracksuit etc. from the bus. She was away for quite a few minutes, but did eventually return with my belongings, having had a job to find it, with many other people sorting through bags which were slung all over the bus.

When I met up with Ian Wooldridge, and a couple of the other lads who had finished, Ian offered me a glass of Champagne, and for some inexplicable reason, I refused. I told myself, that I was a little dehydrated, and alcohol would not be a good idea, at the time. Absolutely logical, but absolutely daft, and something that I look back on with regret. Surely I could have allowed myself a little leeway, in that situation. However, I have now decided, that should anyone offer me Champagne in the future, I will never decline it. As for Bridgette and Dee, they managed to get to about the half way point, before they decided to call it a day, and Andrew Dibsdale finished, a couple of hours after me.

CHAPTER 24

The Start Of The Nineties

A round the late eighties, a gentlemen started to put his style on the management committee of the Transplant Sports Association. His name was Ross Taylor, who was the Transplant Surgeon from Newcastle Freeman Hospital. It was not long before Ross took over as chairman, with Maurice Slapak, given the title of president, which meant that he was still around but the day-to-day job was in the capable hands of Ross. Our new chairman was a people person, who would always have time for everyone. At the Games he would try to get round to every event and speak to as many people as he could. He could always be relied on to make the appropriate speech at the Gala Dinner, on Sunday evening. One thing he always insisted upon was the singing of *You'll never walk alone*, at the end of the night. I am not sure of Ross' sporting background, and he was never one for blowing his own trumpet, but I suspect he was a decent runner in his younger days. I recall running a 1,500 metres race, when Ross was acting as the running partner of a blind transplant runner. Ross must have been in his late fifties when he did this. Ross was a good friend of Brendan Foster, being established in the North East, and was able to call on his help, when the British Transplant Team needed track suits, etc. I was starting to regain some of my previous enthusiasm for running, and in 1991, I was back in the international team. By then it had been decided to move the international games to odd years, which helped to avoid clashes with other major internationals, mainly in respect of raising finance, although we did start to receive money from Europe, for our British team.

The venue was Budapest, in Hungary, but there was a problem, in the form of the old injury to my Achilles tendon. After performing well in the British Games and gaining selection for Budapest, my training had been interrupted by the old injury. I was now a senior competitor, and only a few years off from being a vet. I shared a room with Paul Silcox, who like me had been part of the British team, on and off since New York, in 1980.

We were accommodated at the 'Stadium' hotel, which was across the road from a huge football stadium, and a park that was full of statutes, of obvious revolutionary heroes of the past. The Metro was a few yards from the hotel. We had been told that we were about six stops from the central area of Budapest. Paul and I decided to make the trip to the centre, but we could not work out how you obtained a ticket, although we worked out the cost would be about twelve pence in sterling. When the train arrived we just got on and figured we may be able to pay, when we got off. We had travelled a couple of stops, when an inspector appeared and asked to see our tickets. We tried to explain but he ordered off the train, and requested us to pay a fine, which worked out at about five pounds each, we then carried on our journey. Everything was so cheap over there, at that time, but there seemed to be a lot of poverty, and everywhere people were trying to sell things. One day three of us got a taxi to take us about four or five miles. When we got out the taxi driver asked for about ninety-five pence, in our money, so we gave him about one pound fifty.

Due to the lack of training, through the Achilles tendon problem, I was well below the pace in my two races, and for the first time, had not returned with a medal from an international. Again, in 1995, I made the international team, but this time, we did not have to travel abroad, as the World Games were being held in Manchester. Gill decided she would stay at home as Nicola was close to giving birth to her second child. Lucas, Nicola's first child, who had been born two years earlier, was six weeks early, after a difficult pregnancy. Her second pregnancy was also difficult, and we suspected that the second child would also be born early. I decided to travel up to Manchester, after the opening ceremony, just prior to the competition starting, as I did not want to take too much time off work. The accommodation was at Manchester University Halls of Residence. When I arrived I meet up with some of the British team, many of whom I knew, and they filled me in, on what was happening and where everything was. My Achilles tendon problem flared up just prior to the games. We did have access to physiotherapy at the games themselves, which I took up prior to competing. The mini marathon was taking place in central Manchester. I started to warm up, but took it easy, and could still feel the problem. I started the race, but had only gone about a quarter of a mile, when I had to pull up, and retire from the race. I continued with some physiotherapy, as I kept up hope that I could take part in the 1,500 metres, which was three or four days away. With the transplant games there is always a doctor about to discuss a problem with. In respect of my Achilles problem, after a discussion with our team doctor, they could give me an injection, in my ankle, to numb the pain for a few minutes whilst I ran the race, and would not do any long term damage. There were due to be heats for the 1,500 metres (Vets), but on the Saturday the official decided, they would just have a straight final on the Sunday.

The plan was, I would go to the start, accompanied by my doctor, and just before the race was due to start, I would be given a quick injection, by the Achilles. This is what happened, and I started the race. After about 150 metres, I felt the problem, and although it gave some relief, I virtually limped for the rest of the race, but I wanted to finish which I did. On the Monday morning, just before I was about to travel home, I rang my wife. She told me that Nicola, had given birth to her second child, a boy, Jack, although it had been a difficult birth, and she had to be rushed from Solihull Hospital to Heartlands Hospital. At least I had something to celebrate when I returned home.

CHAPTER 25

The Birmingham Team

The Birmingham Team itself, did ok, over the years, but never good enough to be the top team at the annual games. I was still team manager during the nineties, which basically involved ensuring the entry forms were completed and in on time, and with regard to team events, volleyball and relays, I took charge. We did have some ups, in respect of both, but generally our strength in depth was not there. We did on the odd occasion come second or third in the volleyball tournament, having a couple of decent volleyball players, and a good girl player, named Kay MacDonald. Kay was a good all-round sports women, who competed internationally, in swimming, badminton and also volleyball. Newcastle and Cleveland, were two of the top teams. In one competition we played Cleveland in the semi-finals. It was one of those games were everything went right, I was totally amazed when we won the game by seven points to four. I think we were all gobsmacked, however, we were soon brought down to earth when Newcastle trashed us in the final. On one occasion, we were doing quite well in the volleyball competition, and were due to play our next game. We had a new young lad in our team, who definitely, had an excess of energy. In fact I would put him in the ADHD bracket. When the officials asked for the captains for tossing the coin, before I knew it he was on the court like a flash, won the toss and had given the opposition the service. We were seven nil down before we knew it and inevitably lost the game. Our energetic team mate was not the most popular of individuals, over the weekend.

We were very fortunate to have the services of a gentlemen named Eric McCalla, for a while, in the Birmingham Team. Eric, was a top athlete, he was a seventeen metre plus triple jumper, who had came eight in the Los Angeles Olympics, representing Great Britain. He was a lovely guy, and was keen to avoid events where he would be so dominant that everyone else would be insignificant. However, I needed to use his talents for team events, and he was happy to help out, in that role. Because of his spring when he played in the Volleyball team, he could virtually jump above the net to smack the ball down into the opponent's court. When it came to the 4 x 100 metre relay, I thought that for the first time, with Eric, in the team, we may have a chance of actually winning it. The rules of the relay was that each team had to have one lady. We were fortunate that we had a young girl, named Ka Wai Yap, who was small and slight, but a good sprinter. We also had Dave Edmonds, who was about six foot three, again not a bad runner, but mainly known for being a good badminton player, who had formed an excellent doubles partnership with Keith Bowkett. It was a coincidence that Keith had his transplant on the same day as myself, 8 September, but five years later. When my transplant was twenty years old, and Keith's was fifteen years old we had a joint party, and to this day, I receive a birthday card, on 8 September, from Keith and his wife, Ollie, and Keith receives a card from Gill and myself. Back to the relay, I decided to ask Ka Wai to take the first leg, with Dave being tall to run the back straight. I would run the bend, and Eric would take the final leg. Before the race, as we always did, we had baton changing practice. I always suggested the same way to change the baton, which was basically the front person would hold a straight arm down behind them with their thumb pushed out, leaving a gap for the baton to be lifted into the hand, by the oncoming runner. I cannot recall we ever dropped the baton, using this method of changeover.

I was more concentrating on what was happening in the race, but my wife tells me that when the race started, and Ka Wai was running the first leg, Eric still had his tracksuit on. He then started to do his version of 'the stripper', as Dave did his bit in the back straight and handed over to me. I knew we were still in contention, and gave it my all round the bend. I lifted the baton into Eric hand and he was off down the finishing straight, I think we may have been a couple of yards behind the leader at the changeover, but Eric was in the lead at the tape and we had won our first relay. I was really happy and there were smiles all round as we stood on the rostrum, Dave 6' 3", Ka Wai about 4' 8", with me and Eric in the middle. Eric, unfortunately had a condition where his body attacked his kidney, and over a period of three or four years, was back on dialysis. However, I am happy to report that I saw him recently, and he advised me that he had had a second kidney transplant, which was doing well, and with new medical techniques, I very much hope that his new kidney will be good for many years. He received his new kidney at Wallsgrave Hospital, in Coventry. The downside was, he told me if he competed in future, it may have to be for the Coventry team!

I remember purchasing some new running shoes, which had not long come onto the scene, about this time, and they were regarded as giving a soft landing to your heels, which I was looking for. I will not say the make of this new type of shoe, but you may get a tick for guessing. I usually kept these in the porch. I walked into the porch one day and was immediately hit be a horrible smell which I was convinced was cat pee. When I picked up my trainers, the smell was definitely coming from them. Itwas so bad that I removed them from the porch, threw them in the shed, and soon after disposed of them in the rubbish bin. I did not understand why our cat had taken a dislike to my running shoes, or me for that matter. Many months later I was watching a consumer programme, on television, where they reported that several people had contacted them regarding a problem with this particular type of running shoe. To provide a cushioning, this shoe has an area under the heel, whichcontained a fluid. Many people complained that this area had leaked,rendering the running shoe as faulty. It was also reported that the fluid gave out a very unpleasant smell, something like cat pee. Well there you are. I did apologise to the cat for the accusation, but did not have the shoes to take back to the running shop to get some compensation.

CHAPTER 26

Down Under.

It was 1997, I was 47, and pretty much thinking that international success in the World Transplant Games was a thing of the past, but I kept plugging away, and gained selection again for the British Team, at the domestic games, that year, as a Veteran competitor. This time Sydney, Australia, was the venue, a long way to go to come back with nothing. I had never been to Australia, and would probably not made the effort to do so, if it had not been for the International Games. It was a long journey, and my sister Sandra accompanied my wife and I. We travelled, with the British Team, on Gulf Air, from Heathrow to Bahrain, Bahrain to Singapore, and Singapore to Sydney. Gill, Sandra and I, sat on the back seat. We sat at the back because, my sister smoked, at that time. Throughout the flight people had been coming to the back of the plane to smoke, with Gulf Air being one of the only Airlines, allowing you to smoke at that time. On the last leg, just before we took off, the steward announced, there would be no smoking on board for the final stretch of the flight. There was uproar amongst the people on the plane who wanted to smoke. They said the only reason they choose Gulf Air was because they could smoke. The chief steward then came and spoke to us and asked everyone who wanted to smoke to move to the back of the plane, and everyone at the back of the plane, who did not smoke to stand up. This meant that we would be separated, which we did not want to do on a long haul. There were still a few of us standing up, including the three of us, when the chief steward said he had to go back to the front, or the plane would not be able to take off. Fortunately, a couple of lads, who had been sitting together offered to give up their seats, so we could stay together.

When we arrived at Sydney Airport, we were taken by coach to the outskirts of Sydney, to the Hotel, where we were to stay for the next two weeks. I was sharing a room with one of the team, Edmund Coady, a long term competitor, and Gill shared with Sandra. There were three or four other international teams staying at the hotel. The hotel were very accommodating, and provided a meeting room on the first floor for the British team to use. The hotel was on a busy dual carriageway, almost like a motorway, where the motorists seemed to be very keen on racing. Although, there were pedestrian crossing areas, you needed to keep your wits about you when crossing. On the other side of the road there was a shopping mall, which had eating places, a doctors, dentist and other facilities. Next to the mall, directly opposite from the Hotel, there was a park, which had an area on one side that housed a few trailers. I used the park to run round, on a couple of occasions, as part of my training. On the second occasion, I was running in the park close to some trees, and the next thing I knew, I was being attacked by an Australian magpie. To say it frightened the life out of me, is an understatement, and I ran like a sprinter away from the trees. I was quite shaken up and decided there and then I would be avoiding the park in the future. I was watching the local TV news, a couple of days later, when they showed a postman, on his bike, being attached by another magpie, it seemed it was not an unusual occurrence.

My room, which was on the fourth floor, was at the front of the hotel, facing the park. One day we noticed there was a round hole, about a centimetre in diameter, in the large window, behind one of the curtains. We agreed this looked like a bullet hole. I rang reception and reported the hole. The manager rang me and suggested it could have been a bird hitting the window but he said he would send someone up to have a look. When someone did come to look at it, they seemed to agree with our thinking, and not long after a policeman arrived.

He started looking in the area in front of the hotel directly below my window, presumably for the remains of a bullet. We suspected that if there had been a shot to our window, it would have come from the park opposite, and possibly from the occupants of one of the trailers, but we never had any feedback if they had investigated further.

Sydney was preparing for the 2000 Olympics, which was evident, as we looked around central Sydney. Even though it was three years before the great event they had a large store there that was selling all the goods, relating to event, memorabilia etc., and I did buy a few things to bring back. I was impressed with the city, Central Quay, the restaurants, the harbour bridge, and of course the Opera House. We marched to the Opera House for the opening ceremony, where we listens to the speeches, whilst sitting on the steps of this impressive building. We also travelled by boat from Central Quay to a couple of places. One was Manley Beach, were the British Lions Rugby Team have been known to stay, on their tours. The place had a wealth of fish restaurants and we took advantage of one of them. The other boat trip took us to Taronga Zoo, which was on the other side of the bay. Once you departed the boat you make your way to the top of the hill where the Zoo entrance is. Then the Zoo was on the side of the hill. We made our way down, looking at the animals, including kangaroos, koalas, and a komodo dragon, that was wandering about, until we reached the bottom of the hill, to exit and re-join the boat. The Stadium we were using for the athletics was the old main National Stadium, which was next where the new Olympic Stadium was under construction. The old stadium would be used as a warm up track for the Olympics in 2000. We travelled to this stadium a couple of times for training, prior to the actual competition. The Olympic complex which then could almost be described as a building site, was about forty five minutes coach drive from our hotel. Apart from other sporting venues it was also home to the Aquatics Centre, which would be the venue for swimming and diving, for the Olympics. It was an existing pool, but four thousand extra seats were due to be installed for the Olympics in three years time. We enjoyed watching the transplant swimming event and supporting our British swimmers.

My training in the UK had been restricted by my usual injury problem, but I did manage to get a few weeks injury free prior to going to Australia, and with about a week before competition, once I got to Sydney I was hoping to continue my build up training. This proved to be the case and I did manage to get some good sessions in prior to the competition, remaining injury free. The 800 metres had been added to the list of events for men, in these World Games. I was therefore entered into the 800 metres, 1,500 metres, and the five kilometres (mini marathon). I knew with the mini marathon, being the distance race, that with restricted training my chances of coming in a medal place was slim. As this was my first race, I decided I would start tentatively and see what happened. As I thought that I had more chance in the other two races, because of where I was in training, and did not want to risk a reoccurrence of the Achilles tendon problem. The mini marathon was one race, in Paramatta Park, which covered all age categories; adult, senior, vet, super vet, distinguished by the numbers that runners where wearing. I took it easy at the start of race for the reasons I outlined. I did push myself a bit harder in the later stages of the run, but the lack of distance training showed, and I was not in a medal position. On the day of the track events my first race was the 1,500 metres. I took my place on the start line with about ten other runners, it was a sunny day but not too hot. I had no strategy, just see how the race progressed and take it from there. The starting pistol sounded and we were off. I found myself in front quite quickly, and tried to keep a descent pace going, although I did not know how long I could keep it up. To my amazement I was still ahead on the final lap, having taken the bell. On the back straight I was feeling a bit strained, and attempted to look round, at which point, my team mate Pete, who standing on the side, shouted at me not to look round, and just keep going. As I entered the home straight, a runner from the USA overtook me and I could not respond. Then a Spanish guy also overtook me, this time something pushed me to react, and I managed to overtake him before the line. I had a silver medal and was pretty happy with that after so many years of frustration.

Later in the afternoon the 800 metres took place. I was still on a bit of a high after winning the silver, and had not thought too much about my strategy for this race. I took my place in the lane, which I was sharing with a fellow GB team member, Pedro (his ancestry was Spanish, I think). I would be doing this until we broke from the lanes in the back straight. When the gun went off Pedro shot off quickly, leaving me a little behind. It was a wakeup call, which galvanised me to speed up and compete. As we broke in the back straight I found myself in the lead. I kept a strong pace, in this two lap race, somewhat quicker than the 1,500 metres. The guys in the 800 were pretty much the same as in the 1,500, so I knew there would be competition from the runners from USA, Spain, and possible an 800 metre specialist. On the final back straight, I made no attempt to look round, and kept pushing it round the final bend, and into the home straight. I was expecting a challenge at anytime but it never happened, and I crossed the line ahead of the field. The next day I was presented with a gold and silver medal at the stadium.

Our stay in Sydney was for two weeks before we returned home. Many of our group, had booked a third week, and travelled up to Cairns, to visit the Great Barrier Reef. In hindsight I wish now I had done this, as Australia is a long way to travel, which I may not do again, and it would have been a good opportunity to visit this amazing area. We did manage a trip to the Blue Mountains, by train. They are about sixty miles away from Sydney. We travelled on a train that had seating on two levels, which cost about four pounds (sterling) return (slightly less than British Rail would charge for this distance). The Blue Mountains are so called because of the blue haze that is created by the eucalyptus trees, the leaves of which are the staple diet of the koala bears. The day we travelled to the Blue Mountains was very wet, which probably affected the look of the area, but I can imagine it being very impressive in the right conditions.

The journey back home took about thirty-one hours. We flew from Sydney to Melbourne, then to Singapore, then Bahrain, getting off the plane, at each for about an hour and a half to two hours. If we decide to travel to Australia, or New Zealand in future, I intend to stay over at Singapore, or a mid-point for a couple of days to break the journey, although I think the flying down under is more efficient these days.

CHAPTER 27

Birmingham's Turn

We were getting close to the end of century, and it was very clear to me that Ross Taylor, the current and much respected chairman of the Transplant Sports Association of Great Britain, was very passionate about holding the first transplant games, of the new century, in his adopted city of Newcastle. He had a little problem because up to this point we did not have a bid for 1999. From a conversation I had with him one day, I had the definite impression that Ross was cajoling me to think about offering Birmingham, for this slot. It had been almost twenty years since Birmingham had been the host of the games, in 1980. I was now the only active member, from Birmingham, on the management committee. Tony Barnes was still a trustee, but had taken a back seat, in recent years, and Malcolm Simms had not been on the committee for some years, so if Birmingham were to bid for 1999, it was going to be up to me to get things moving. I arranged a meeting with Tony Barnes at the Queen Elizabeth Hospital, and as usual he was his friendly and helpful self, but I got the impression, although supportive, he would not be actively involved in the organisation for the next Birmingham Games. He was getting close to retirement, moving to Wales and concentrating on his fly fishing, which after his illustrious career, who could deny him. The Queen Elizabeth Hospital was now a Transplant Hospital for Hearts and Livers, as well as kidneys. All these departments now had their own heads, and my next step was to write to them all to gain their support for the venture. My other objective in writing to these Heads, was to try and find a transplant consultant who would be prepared to be actively involved in the organisation. This would also be necessary, because the normal practise was that the chairperson of the local organising committee would be a transplant consultant from the host unit.

I received a positive response from all the Heads of Departments, and also a name was advised of one of the transplant surgeons who would be interested in being actively involved. Her name was Laura Buist, who was a consultant renal transplant surgeon, originally from Scotland with an interest in sport. I arranged an initial meeting, asking all people who may be interested, in getting involved, to attend. The meeting was not well attended but we did have some useful people there including Laura Buist, and a lady named Brenda Norris, who had been involved in the organisation of the Birmingham Games in 1980, and a representative from Birmingham City Council's Sport Department. I outlined the background of the Transplant Games, for those people who were not too familiar, and advised that we needed to put a paper together, our bid for submission to the management committee, to get the go ahead to host the Games in 1999. The bid would need to include some basic information with regard to sporting venues, accommodation, funding, transport etc. At the next meeting, I said we also needed to select suitable members to be the local organising committee for the Birmingham games.

Working for Birmingham Council at that time, was useful because of the contacts I had, and the knowledge of many of the council sporting facilities. I had some initial thoughts, and if we were able to book early enough, and choose the right dates, suitable sporting facilities could be found. The athletics stadium I wanted was Alexander Stadium, the home of Birchfield Harriers, and only four or five miles from the city centre, and then emerging as one of the top athletic venues in the country. We had Highgate, which was a Sports Hall, very close to the city centre, suitable for Volleyball, Badminton, Table Tennis etc. There was, and still is not a 50 metre swimming pool, in Birmingham, which sadly was the case for many Transplant Game's venues. We did have some decent 25 metres pools, and selected Stetchford Cascades. In terms of accommodation, the Games usually offered a combination of hotels and university halls of residence. I managed to get an idea of rates from city centre hotels, and also get some preferable rates from Birmingham University.

At our next meeting, I proposed Laura Buist as our chair, which was carried. Brenda would be our secretary, and a fellow transplant recipient, Dennis Tye, who took part in the games, was elected treasurer. Dennis was an accountant by profession, and ran his own business. I knew Dennis well, and was happy with his appointment to this responsible position. I drafted the bid, with Laura's support, and at the next management committee meeting put it on the table for consideration. After some questions to myself from committee members, it was proposed by Brian Hall, that the bid should be accepted. This was voted upon, and Birmingham were given the go ahead to host the 1999 Transplant Games.

In 1998, the British Games were held in Belfast, and as well as competing and being team manager, I used the visit to liaise with their organising people. Laura Buist also travelled with the team. It was helpful for her to have attended a Games prior to the Birmingham Games. It would be useful to be able to get feedback from them on such things as numbers attending, number of people in individual events, up to date names of team managers, amount of merchandise sold, etc. They were very helpful in this regard as we finalised our plans over the next few months. Laura had found a lady who would work for us, at a reasonable rate to process all the entry forms, including all the event entries, and accommodation requirements, and social event requirement. The was quite a sizable task with the number of people now attending the Games, and could only be achieved by having someone committed for many hours before and during the Games. There was software available, which had been developed through the management committee, over the years.

In terms of numbers, we required a venue for the Sunday Evening Gala Dinner that would be able to cope with twelve hundred people for a sit down meal. The only place I knew locally that would be able to provide this was the Metropole Hotel, at the NEC, where I had spent my wedding night, and my step-daughter Nicola had her wedding reception. I knew that the Metropole had a room that would accommodate this number of diners, it was called the Monarch suite. It was free the evening we required it, so I made sure that we had the room booked, and secured. The members of the committee all had specific roles, my main one was transportation, but I seemed to get involved in most of the organisation. The problem areas were mainly to do with the venues and running of the less mainstream sports, which had come to be included over the years. Ten Pin bowling was a case in point. As with most of the events, I had booked the venue as early as possible, to make sure we did not miss out, through availability. I had dealt with a person, at the Stirchley Ten Pin Bowling Centre, and booked the evening we required. About three months before the day, I popped in to discuss and finalise the arrangements. The person I had dealt with had left, and there was no record of the booking. Luckily they could still accommodate us on the evening we required, and were very helpful.

We had Snooker and Darts, as social events. I found a Snooker Hall where we were able to run the competition, and also came across a helpful guy who offered to run the event for us. Canoeing had been a recent inclusion in the Games, which initially was a problem area. I had found a place to hold it, but all the arrangement needed to handled by ourselves, and with no expertise this was going to be difficult. I was getting pretty desperate when my friend, Brian Cole, who worked at Land Rover, put me in contact with a couple of guys who worked there, who were greatly involved in canoeing. When I approached them, they said 'no problem', and I left to them to it, and they did a great job. I think the biggest problem for me was the cycling event. I wanted to use Sutton Park, but this was not possible, and my contacts in the Sports section, of Birmingham Council, suggested a couple of parks in the City. I was not particularly happy with either from a safety point of view, but with no other alternative, we plumped for one of them. The one we choose had a lake in the centre, which was close to the pathway, at one point. My worst feared were founded when on first lap one of the cyclist ended up in the water, luckily one of the helpers from Birmingham Council, was close by and fished him out quickly, although he did have a badly gashed leg.

In terms of transportation I was very fortunate to have found a guy in one of the Council departments who had recently handled the transport of a major international event. He not only advised me what he thought would be the best way to organise the transportation, he came to some meetings to provide support. His advice was to use the local bus provider, 'West Midlands Transport', and use a hub system, where all the transport went back to a central point. When West Midlands Transport costed our requirements, they quoted less that we had in the budget for transportation, and provided us with a manager who was around for the whole of the three days.

We even had a bendy bus, as one of the buses used to transport people the Metropole for the Gala Dinner. I personally decided I could not compete in the Birmingham Games and also be an organiser over the three/four days, of the event. I drove a mini bus, as a supplement to the West Midlands Transport System, as did a friend of mine who also worked for Birmingham Council. The two mini buses were donated, through a contact that we had. The mini buses gave us flexibility, and allowed us to transport the odd individually who needed to get from one event to another, which could not be catered for via the main transport operation.

Generally the organisation went well and there were no major problems. The social events had been well received, including the Saturday night at the Halls of Residence at Birmingham University, where we had an evening we called the 'Brummie Night'. There was a meal laid on, and the entertainment was provided by Malcolm Stent, and his band. Malcolm was a local comedian and singer, who provided a great night's entertainment. Whilst doing his act, Chris Evans, the Transplant Surgeon, from Liverpool, walked past, and Malcolm recognised her. He had seen her a few nights before on television. Chris was a regular on television, as she was involved with various surgery, related to people who have had renal failure, including some that helped with impotency. For the next few minutes Malcolm had some amusing banter with her, which brought much laughter from the attending audience.

Sunday was the Athletics day, which was taking place at Alexander Stadium. Again the organisation went well, and the programme ran fairly smoothly. The only problem was the weather, as the heavens opened for most of the day. The allocation of seating for the Gala Dinner on the Sunday, was always going to be a challenge. Tables were a certain size and teams wished to sit together, but numbers from team to team could vary from a couple of people to thirty plus people. I had co-opted, my wife Gill to help out with some of the social events, and we were both getting a bit stressed about the Gala Dinner. I decided to ask my step-son, Theron, to provide a plan of where everyone one would sit for the evening. He worked for Land Rover, in logistics, and was able to come up with a plan, which I passed on to the Catering Manager, at the Metropole, a couple of days before. We were even more stressed out when on the way to the Gala Dinner, I suddenly realised that I had not told Theron, to include a party of people who had been invited to the evening, for supporting the event. When we arrived I made a bee line for the Catering Manager, and told him of my omission. When he said to me he had included an extra table, as in large events such as these, there are often some people, who get forgotten, I could have kissed him. We in Birmingham had done our bit, and I was pleased that it went pretty well, although my fellow organisers, and myself did have a few stressful moments.

The early days of the Transplant Games, had plenty of national publicity, which the media seems to give when something is in its infancy. Through research that had been carried out, it appeared that there was an increase in the region of where the Transplant Games take place each year, of people who register for the donor scheme, and carry the card. In 2000, Ross Taylor's wish came true and the first transplant games of the twenty-first century was staged in Newcastle upon Tyne. Ross wanted it to be the best transplant games ever and called upon all his contacts, and energy for this to happen. Through his friendship with Brendan

Foster, he was able to get Steve Cram to do some commentating at the Athletics, and Jonathon Edwards and his family, attended the Gala Dinner. This was just prior to Jonathan travelling to Sydney, to win his Olympic Gold Medal, in the triple jump. We used Gateshead Stadium, which now regularly catered for international athletic events, having benefited from the legacy of Brendan Foster enormous impact on Tyneside.

Later that year I took part in the Great North Run, the half marathon that started in Newcastle, over the Tyne Bridge, and on to South Shields by the coast. There were thirty-six thousand, that year, more than the London Marathon. It took me about twenty minutes to get passed the start, having placed myself in the masses, with the runners who expected to do about two hours for the run. It was an amazing event, where, for the whole of the run, I was surrounded by hundreds of people. In 2013, there were 55,000 runners, which makes you think how many more people can mass runs such as Great North Run and the London Marathon cope with. I did not run particularly well, but I enjoyed the experience, up in the North East.

I was coming up for re-election for the management committee, again, in 2001, and after being on the committee for twenty years decided that I was not going to put myself forward. I was also that it was getting to a point where my participation in the games, would end. I had reached my half century, and really did not see myself has competing any more. I had managed to find someone to take over the Birmingham Team Manager role, which was my only other concern. In 2005, I was invited down to London, for a Dinner at the Dorchester Hotel. It was organised by a Transplant Surgeon from up north. Everyone in the UK who had a functioning transplanted kidney, for twenty-five years and over was invited. There were about four hundred people who came into this category. Around one hundred and fifty kidney recipients actually attended this dinner, some of whom I knew from the early days of the Transplant Games, who I had not seen for many years. At that time there were still people who had functioning transplanted kidneys, for over forty years.

CHAPTER 28

A Little Concern

After my kidney transplant, when things had settled down, my hospital appointments reduced gradually, to a frequency of twice a year. I had a choice of attending my outpatients appointments at either the Queen Elizabeth Hospital, or Heartlands Hospital (previously known as East Birmingham Hospital). I decided to choose Heartlands, as it was closer to where I worked, which, at that time was Alcan Plate Limited, based in Kitts Green, Birmingham.

I did see a variety of Doctors, Consultant's and Registrars, at the outpatients' clinics, although in the early days, I regularly saw Dr Hawkins, who I always had the greatest respect for. I remember he attended one of the Quiz Nights, with his family, which I ran to raise some funds for myself or one of the other local transplant competitors to compete in the International Games.

In early 2008, I went to my usual six monthly check up, and saw a lady consultant, who I had not encountered before. The usual routine, was a quick chat on how I had been doing, sometimes a quick examination, and then I was given some forms to give to the phlebotomist, in the section where blood was taken. A few days later I would get a copy of the letter that would be sent to my GP, for their records, usually saying all was well. On this occasion a couple of days later, I received a phone call from the Hospital saying that my blood results, were of concern and they wanted me to have a scan, which they would arrange. I heard nothing more, and a few days later I received a letter giving me an appointment for my usual six months hence. Thinking that there must have been a mistake with the phone call, and naively, and probably optimistically, I did not query the phone call, and just put it behind me. When, six months later, I attended my next appointment, the Consultant, I saw, who I had not met before, confirmed that blood results from the last visit were not as good as usual. I explained the situation, and he could not understand why a scan had not been arranged for me. He investigated, but his main concern was to get a scan done as soon as possible. When a scan was done, it suggested that the transplanted kidney, itself, was fine, but it showed there was a blockage in the Urethra, which is the tube, that takes urine from the kidney to the bladder. It is part of the re-plumbing that takes place, in a kidney transplant operation. Somehow my medical support would need to find a way to unblock it.

At this time, I had been working for Aston Martin, in Non Production Purchasing for about six years, always on the basis of a contractor. It was a bad time for the car industry, with Aston Martin being particularly hard hit by poor sales. One day the entire workforce at our Gaydon manufacturing plant were asked to attend a mass meeting, by senior management. At the meeting we were advised the gravity of the situation, and told that 300 contractors, and 300 permanent employees would be leaving. As there were just over 300 contractors employed at the company, I knew that my job was in serious jeopardy, and within two weeks, myself many other contractors, found ourselves unemployed. As it worked out over the next few months I found myself in and out of hospital, due to the problem with the Urethra being blocked, and therefore, as a contractor, I could not have carried out the role.

I was referred back to the Queen Elizabeth Hospital, but not to the Transplant Unit, which I expected, but to the Urology department. A procedure was booked for me, which involved inserting a line into a vein, via the kidney and into the Urethra, and hopefully through to the bladder, thus clearing the blockage. After a few attempts, the doctor attempting to do this admitted defeat, and advised me that it could not be done this way. His original comment to me had been hopefully, once this was done, I could look forward to another thirty years, of good health. The problem was that they were struggling to understand how my transplant operation had been carried out, with regard to the connection of the Urethra to the bladder. Because my operation was thirty years before, the surgeon who did it, Mr Mathieson, was long gone, and also other surgeons, around at that time, who would have used similar techniques, would have also retired, or moved on.

I was then referred to the Transplant Unit, itself and shortly afterwards I received an appointment to see a transplant surgeon. My visit with the surgeon went well and once he had read my notes, I enquired what he intended to do, and in a positive manner he said he would operate. He would open me up using the same line as my original transplant operation, he would then disconnect the Urethra, unblock it, and re-attach it to my bladder. I asked when this would happen, and he advised 'pretty quickly'.

There was a problem at this time. This being that I was starting to get infections, due to the deterioration of my condition. These infection caused me to have high temperatures, which gave the transplant unit a problem, in as much as they would not operate whilst, due to the infection, my temperature was high. On a couple of occasions, I was scheduled for the surgery, but when I was checked out at the hospital, the day before the operation, was due, I was sent home with antibiotics, as an infection was found. This had been a concern, for my Surgeon, and for myself. The next occasion this happened, was a Monday. The intention was that if I was free from infection, the operation would take place on the Tuesday. My temperature was higher than normal, and my blood results showed again that I still had an infection. After discussions with his colleagues, my surgeon spoke to me, and advised that the plan was to keep me in the ward, give me a course of antibiotics, and look to operate on Friday. He advised me, that this depended on one or two things falling into place. Firstly, that my temperature had fallen, secondly he had a complicated operation to carry out on Friday morning and it depended on how long that took, whether they could fit me in, as the operating theatre was usually closed in the afternoon. When it came to Friday morning, the first part of the equation fell into place, in that my temperature was around normal. No one had said anything to me in the morning, and when 12 noon approached, I was becoming resigned to the fact that the operation was not going to happen that day. At 12.30pm, a theatre operative arrived, and announced he had come to take me for my operation. When I was wheeled in through the doors, a jovial Anaesthetist, greeted me and stated that he would be off home by now if it was not for me, but he did have a smile on his face, and I thanked him. When I woke after the operation my surgeon was there and he said the operation went well and he was happy with the result.

My hospital stay, after the operation was not long, but my Surgeon, was insistent, that the catheter, should remain in place for as long as possible, to allow the joining of the Urethra to the bladder to heal. However, as you will know, if you have ever had to endure a catheter for any length of time, that it is not a pleasant experience, and is something you push to be extracted. Whilst in hospital a few weeks later for some tests, I put some pressure on one of my Surgeons team to take the catheter out. In the absence of my Surgeon, his junior made the decision to remove the catheter, as he thought that the healing process would have happened. A few days later, I was at my GPs, seeing a nurse, who was attending to my dressing. She was alarmed when removing the dressing, that there was a leakage, from the wound. She was quite concerned and immediately contacted the Queen Elizabeth Hospital, who said I should go back straight away. When I saw my Surgeon he again reiterated that I needed to have the catheter back in, as it took the pressure off the newly joined Urethra, and allowed the seal to fully heal. The catheter was re-inserted and I realised for the next few weeks, I would have to accept this was the case. Once he was fully satisfied that the healing process was complete, my Surgeon, gave his authority for the catheter to be removed. With the repair now fully healed, and my blood results improved, I was now in a position, to look for a return to employment, if I could find a job.

I had been out of work for about nine months, even when I left the Police Force, I had only been unemployed for about two weeks. At the age of fifty-nine I was not confident of finding work, although I thought, because of my experience with Birmingham City Council, Procurement work related to the public sector was my best hope. Searching online, my wife, Gill, came across an opportunity, being advertised by an agency. She asked me if it was something what was suitable for me. When I studied the detail, it appeared that a further education establishment, where looking for someone with 'Public Sector' procurement experience. Although it did not say, I assumed that the vacancy was at Aston University, in the centre of Birmingham. If this was the case then I would certainly be interested. I emailed my updated CV to the agency, and enquired if I would be of interest for this position. The next day I received a phone, from the agency, and after a short conversation, they said, they thought, I would suitable, and they would pass my details, onto the University. Within a couple of days, the agency, came back to me, and said that the University would like me to go for an interview, the following week. They also said the person, who was looking to recruit, had previously worked with me at Aston Martin. When I enquired what his name was, they told me 'Adrian Owen'.

The name Adrian Owen, did not ring a bell with me. I could not think of anyone, in Procurement, at Aston Martin, with that name. After a further conversation, with the agency, they advised that Adrian Owen, had worked in the Finance Department of Aston Martin. I then realised who he was, and I remembered that I had had some dealing with him, and had found him to be a decent guy. When I went to the interview, Adrian introduced a lady, who was the Purchasing Manager. He said that the job would be working for him, in the University's Estates Department, but would have a dotted line to the Purchasing Manager, who was in charge of Central Purchasing. He explained that the job initially would be as a contractor, but there was the possibility that the job could be made permanent, at some point. They were also interviewing another person, who had been sent by the same employment agency. Adrian advised they would let me know as soon as possible, and I confirmed that I would very interested, in the position, if offered. The next day the agency rang to say they were offering me the job.

The Estates Office I was working in, had mix of professions, including Engineers, an Environmental Section, people who looked after the use of space (very important in a University Establishment), plus Arian's section, which was concerned with the Estate's Finances. My first priority was to pick up the setting up of Framework Contracts, for Electrical, Mechanical, and Minor Building requirements. Frameworks provide companies, who have gone through a procurement process, to be used for work, as required, around the University. The previous Purchasing Officer, in Estates, had left suddenly, and these Frameworks needed to set up without delay. Also there was a programme of capital development being embarked on, at Aston University, and because of Public Procurement legislation, it was something that I would be heavily involved in, as the Estate's Purchasing Officer.

I got on well with Adrian, as I did with the other people within the Estates Department, and generally enjoyed the role, although it could be stressful at times. After about six months my position was made permanent, after a process. My role did change to some extent, in that Central Procurement, wanted me to report to them, with a dotted line to Adrian, although, for the majority of the time I was still based in the Estates Department. One of the benefits of working at somewhere like a University, is that there is usually access to facilities, such as a sports centre, and swimming pool, which was the case at Aston. There were also some running enthusiasts who started a running group, during the time I was working there. Whether you were an out and out beginner, or a regular runner you were welcome in to join the group. They welcomed beginners and used a programme to move from being able to jog a couple of hundred yards, to jogging no stop for three miles, within about ten to twelve weeks. I had not run for years, so I happy to join the beginners group and gradually follow the programme.

Initially, I progressed along with my fellow 'beginners', and was soon able to take on a three mile run for Red Nose Day, in Solihull. My time was pretty slow, but I did manage to keep going all the way. I was starting to have injury problems. In my competitive days, I did have problems with my Achilles tendon from time to time, as recorded previously in this book, but generally very little else in the way of injuries. Now, quite a few more areas of my body started to complain about my return to pounding along hard canal sides, etc. Firstly my heel was painful, a condition, which a fellow jogger advised that my injury was called 'Plantar Fasciitis' commonly known as Joggers Heel. It occurs when the thick band of tissue, that runs underneath your foot, from your heal bone to the toes becomes inflamed. Then my Achilles flared up again, followed by a problem with my knee, which may have been cartilage, but was never actually diagnosed, and then a hamstring injury, usually associated with sprinters. Technically speaking I was a physical wreck, when it came to my condition for running. I visited my physiotherapist, who had provided treatment for my Achilles in my younger days, a few times for help with these additional problems. When I told him that I had acquired a bike, and was curtailing the running, he said, "I think that's a good idea!" To be honest, not accounting for the injury problems, I had found the return to running hard, which I basically put down to not getting any younger. This may be the case, but it may be that other areas of my health may have had some bearing on this, which I refer to a little later in my story. There will not be any more mention of the use of my bike, as it was seldom used either, though we do have many bike lanes around where we live, I am still happier with contact with the ground, as my form of exercise.

CHAPTER 29

The Torch

It was 2011 and the London Olympics were on the horizon. Information about the torch relay was being publicised in the summer. After a family discussion, where I said it was something I would love to do, and my daughter-in-law, Louise said she would be happy to nominate me. Louise was Theron's wife. They were married in 1995, and their son Jonathan was born in 2001. Louise was the ideal person to put forward a nomination, as her career background was in PR, and she was very good at delivering a message in the right manner. She nominated me online through the direct Olympic site. There were other nomination routes one of them being Lloyd TSB Bank. I understood that 8,000 people would be carrying the torch, throughout the UK. (I later understood 7,300, were through nomination, with 700 allocated to sports people and celebrities.)

In September 2011, I received an email from the Olympic organisers, with basically said, 'Congratulations, you have reached the second round'. The bad news was that it also said that, I had reached the second round with about 28,000 other people, and there were 2,000 places available. I assumed the other 6,000 places where allocated through Lloyds TSB, and the other organisations. With 28,000 nominations on the table, and 2,000 places, I worked out without the use of a calculator, that I had a fourteen to one chance of carrying the torch. Then, it was reported that Seb Coe had said that fifty percent of the torch bearers would be 25 or under. Putting this into the equation, and I reckoned my chances, were more like twenty-eight to one. For that reason I was not getting too excited, at that stage. In mid December I received an email saying, that subject to certain security checks I would be carrying the Olympic torch. It also said that I should not advise the media, or publicise it, until it was confirmed officially that I would be a torch bearer.

I did tell the family, and manager at work, but asked her not tell anyone until it was confirmed. I was then working at Aston University, close to the centre of Birmingham. I had left Birmingham Council, in 2001, when our department was merging with another department. If I wanted to go, they would let me leave with extra pension years, and a pension immediately, which I decided to take. At that time if you were over fifty, and the council were prepared to let you go, they could offer you early retirement. Shortly after this the rules changed, and early retirement was not available. When I left Birmingham Council, I started work at Land Rover, Gaydon, as a contractor standing in for maternity leave for six months. After this the Purchasing Director, at Land Rover, asked me if I would be interested in working at Aston Martin, on the same Gaydon site, which was then a part of the same group. As a contractor I worked at Aston Martin for another six years, but in 2008, with a downturn in the car market, the company announced they needed to lose 300 Contractors, and 300 permanent staff, and I left at that time.

This coincided with a deterioration of my blood results, which turned out to be a blockage in the urethra, the tube that goes from the kidney to the bladder, which is re-engineered with a kidney transplant. After certain techniques were tried at the Queen Elizabeth, to unblock it without surgery, It was decided that an operation was necessary. In the summer of 2009, I had an operation, were the urethra was disconnected from my bladder, unblocked and reconnected. Although I had some problems, for a while, as detailed previously, the operation was successful, and my blood results soon returned to their normal levels. In October 2009, I joined Aston University, as a Purchasing Officer, in the Estates Department.

In March 2012 the email came through to confirm that I was now officially a torch bearer. Again they asked that I did not publicise the fact. It advised there was to be a launch day, a few days hence when all the torch bearers would be announced. The launch day was on a Monday. The week before I was contacted by the BBC to say that some local torch bearers, myself included, were being asked to take part in a film, prior to the day, for the footage to be used on the Monday launch day. I was also asked to go on local radio, in Coventry, live on the Monday morning, with Louise. Coventry seemed appropriate, as the torches themselves were manufactured in Coventry. The local BBC asked if they could come and film me, on the Friday. As I was at work, I asked permission from our Marketing Department of the University, to do this. Unsurprisingly, they were happy for this to happen, but asked If I could make sure that the Aston University sign was shown when I was being filmed. I also spoke to some of my colleagues in the department, who at that time, I had not told about the torch. Although most people knew I had a kidney transplant, most people did not know about my sporting background. I did not want them to see me being filmed, without telling them first what it was all about.

When the BBC man arrived with his camera and tripod, we had a discussion about how best to do the interview. I told him I had a track suit and trainers with me, as there was a jogging club at the University, I had been involved with. He said it would be good to do some action shots, and then he would film me answering a few questions. There was a small lake on campus, which had a central fountain, where he initially filmed me jogging round, and was happy with, and then we moved to the front of the main entrance of the University, where he prepared to film. It was a cloudy day where the sky was changing quite quickly. He asked me a question, and told me to look at him, not the camera. I proceeded to answer the question on camera. Just when I completed answering his first couple of questions, quite well I thought, the sky changed, and my interviewer said, "Sorry, I need to adjust the camera". Having done this we started again, and he asked me the same question. I got so far again, when some old colleagues from Birmingham Council passed by, they recognised me and waved, which totally threw meand I had to say, "Sorry, could we start again".

When we resumed answering the same question for the third time, I was struggling, and was not sure what I said. When the piece was shown on the Monday, together with about three or four bits about other torch bearers from the Midlands, they showed a couple of things that I said, together with a bit of jogging, and it looked ok. I was asked if I wished to purchase the Torch at a cost of £195, which I decided to do. Closer to the time I received an email from my local authority, offering to buy the torch, or reimburse me, if I had already paid for it. I did think that this was good, as I was in a position to afford the torch, but some torch bearers might not be in that position, and that would be a shame if they were not to keep it. I understand the actual cost of the torch was £495, from the Coventry manufacturer. I was advised that I would be carrying in the torch, in Leamington Spa, which is about three miles from where I now live in Warwick. I did not know have far you ran with the torch. I originally thought it would be about a mile, but later found out that in fact most people carried it for about 300 metres. When I was given the details, of my slot, I was informed that it would be on Sunday 1 July, about 5pm in the afternoon. It was the day that the torch was starting in Birmingham, going through Solihull, Earlswood, Stratford-upon-Avon, Warwick, Leamington Spa, and finishing in Coventry. I would be starting in Spencer Street, run about twenty yards, and then into the Parade, and up to Leamington Spa Town Hall where I would pass the flame onto the next torch bearer.

Although I did work for Estates, at the University, I also worked for Central Procurement, and the week I was due to carry the torch, I was surprised with a cake, showing the Olympic rings, and some nice words from my manager from Procurement, on the Thursday. On the Friday, another cake arrived with a torch on top, made by the wife of the manager of the Estate's department. Both were very much appreciated and tasted very nice. My white torch bearer outfit, also arrived the week before the day, and more or less fit, when I tried it on. I was now ready for the day with some excitement. On either side of the Parade in Leamington Spa, there are parks, where the local council announced they would be running events throughout the afternoon running up to the arrival of the torch. All that was needed was some good weather and hopefully there would be a good turnout. A colleague at work had picked up that the torch was being shown live, through a BBC link. The fact that we had relatives aboard, would mean they could hopefully see me carrying the torch live. Gill's brother, Brian and his family live near Detroit, in Michigan, USA, her sister and husband, Carole and Neville, live in Montreal, Canada, and her younger sister and husband, Shirley and John, live on the Orkneys.

The day arrived, I got dressed in my white outfit, and Gill took a few photos, one with me holding the little torch, from the cake, which the wife of my colleague, at work had made. My instructions were to make my way to a school, in Myton Road, Warwick, and be there at 1.00pm. I dropped Gill in Leamington, and drove to the school, and parked up, about 12.45pm. There were two things going on that day, the Lord's Traveners were playing, and they happened to be using the school, as well as the torch relay. I was not sure if I was at the right school, as there are two schools in Myton Road.

There was a lad on the car park entrance, but he did not know anything about the torch. I was getting slightly concerned until I spotted a couple of other people wearing the same white outfit, as myself. One was a teenage girl from Rugby, who was with her parents, and the other was a guy about fifty. We all had the same question, were we at the right school. The other school was about half a mile down the road. We decided to all walk down to the next school, and ask. As we walked down Myton Road, which is opposite the park area, by the river Avon, we had a few curious looks, from the people who were around at the time. When we reached the other school, we spoke to a couple of lads who were looking after the car park there, again, they had no knowledge of the torch.

The teenage girl's dad said, "I think it's the other school, it seems to be better suited for car parking etc." We all agreed and marched backed to the first school, getting some more curious looks. When we got back there were a couple more people there similarly dressed. We then located a small note on a door at the front of the School. We were at the right place and could go in, which we did. Shortly after a few people from the torch organisation arrived and explained what would happen. There was no rush, the coach to take to where we would be carrying the torch would arrive soon, but would take us altogether about three o'clock. One of the guys asked us to come up individually so he could check his list. There were about eighteen of us. We were given numbers which represented the position were carrying the torch in. I was number '130', the one hundred and thirtieth person to carry the torch on Sunday I July. A torch was shown to us, and also we were given instruction of how to hold it. The weather was good, it was a bright and warm day, ideal for the occasion. The time came for us to board the coach. As we walked on the coach we passed all the torches, standing up on a rack at the front on the left. We drove through Warwick to the starting point for the torch in our area. There were a few people about then, getting ready to watch the torch relay. We parked up for a while waiting for the procession which was on its way from Stratford-upon-Avon. People were walking passed the coach and some spotted the torches, and ourselves waiting to carry them, which produced much pointing, especially when children were in tow. The torch was not carried continuously, but driven from each area to the next, or in some regions a boat, or even a train, as happened when it travelled a few miles on the Severn Valley Railway, were used.

Eventually the procession arrived and we were off to join in. We then went a short distance and the first person in our group was summoned to the front of the bus, given her torch, and disembarked, with good luck wishes from the rest of us. The system was that Police motorcyclists were at the front, when they came to you as a torch bearer, you knew the proceeding torch bearer, was just behind and you were ready to take the flame, the kiss, at it is called, and then you are off for your big moment. The Metropolitan Police Officers who run alongside you, advise how to exchange the flame, when you take it and pass it on to the next person. Once you have finished your run, you are picked up by a second coach, which carries all the people who have completed their slots.

The procession consisted of several vehicles; Lloyds TSB, Samsung, Coca Cola, and the police motorcyclists. Once we had dropped off the first few people, we drove into the private area of Warwick Castle, and stopped in a central area. We were surrounded by trees, and the sun was shining brightly. We were told we were a little ahead of schedule and could get off the bus for a few minutes. Some of us made our way to get a drink from the Coca Cola vehicle. The police motorcycles were all together, and the policemen asked if they could get a few photos of us by the bikes. A couple of the girls mounted the bikes and everyone gathered round, for the police to take their pictures. Back on the coach the people who were carrying the torch, in the grounds of Warwick Castle, were dropped off. We then drove through Warwick High Street, which was packed with onlookers. The coach then made it way to the bridge crossing the Avon. This area had barriers either side where hundreds of people had gathered. The bridge itself was empty and cordoned off, presumably the police were worried that if too many people were on it at any one time it could compromise the bridge. We crossed the bridge, drove down to the island, and turned left into Myton Road. The procession was moving slowly, and almost stopped by the school, where we had boarded the coach. I looked out of the window, and a few feet away standing on the pavement was Seb Coe. I tentatively put my hand up and waved, he smiled, everyone on the coach was making the same comment, "There's Seb Coe".

I found out later that he had been attending the Lord's Taverners Cricket match. Just a coincidence that it was on the same day as the Torch Relay, I assume. The last person to carry the torch in Warwick, was dropped off in Myton Road, before we drove about half a mile to start the Leamington Spa section. One of the torch bearers on the coach suggested that each torch carrier did the 'Usain Bolt – Point', as they got off the coach. We weren't impressed by the first couple of people who did it. The first person to carry the torch in Leamington

Spa, was a teenage lad. He was dropped off in front of the Railway Station, I was the next to be dropped off in Spencer Street. I was handed my torch, got off the coach and did a quick 'Usain Bolt'. There were quite a few people about, but someone told me there were large numbers of people round the corner in the Parade. Before I knew it there was a police motor cyclist heading for me, followed closely by the first Leamington Torch bearer. One of the police women advised us how to put the torches together, to exchange the flame. Once this was done she said I could go, but take it easy as we were ahead of schedule time wise. As I turned the corner, into the Parade, I was amazed at the amount of people. There must have been about ten people deep on each side, and the gap was getting narrower for me to run through. The police on either side of me shouted for people to allow room for us to pass through. The whole thing was a bit surreal, all I could do was smile as much as possible, and hold the torch, as I had been shown. We passed the Pump Room, on my right, which was the home of the 'Spa' treatment, which Leamington had been famous for. I heard my name called a few times, which was from relatives and friends, some of whom I spotted, and acknowledged, as I was jogging along. The Town Hall was coming up on my left, and I could see the young girl, I was passing the flame onto, who was a carer for her mother. Again the police women assisted us, and moved us a little to make sure we could be seen by a camera man, who was located on the balcony of the Town Hall. A few seconds later a coach pulled up and picked me up, and I joined the other torch bearers who had completed their runs. My fellow torch bearers were a cross section of ages and backgrounds. There were teenagers, who were good at sports, or were involved in sport in some way, a man about my age for ran a shelter for people on the streets, a retired British athlete, a man who had raised hundreds of thousands for prostate cancer testing, and a girl who was a carer for her disabled mother. When we eventually returned to the school, we were told that it would take about twenty minutes or so for the torches to have the gas removed, and then they would be handed to us. There were some media people there and they interviewed some of us. We were then handed our torches one by one, and were able to leave. I made my way back close to where I had run, and parked up by the park, alongside the Pump Room. Most of the people lining the parade had now disappeared. I met up with my wife, and a few friends and family, and some photos were taken, including ones with the grandsons, Lucas, Jack, and Jonathan. There were also some people from the St John Ambulance who came over. They said they had been there all day but not managed to see anything, and asked if they could have a picture taken with the torch, which I was quite happy to do. They were also a few people about who spotted what was going on, and made the same request. A very memorable day, and I had an Olympic Torch to take home as an invaluable keepsake.

CHAPTER 30

Into My Sixties

My intention was always to retire from full-time work, in my mid-sixties, finances permitting. I had worked, since I was sixteen, with the only absence from this of any significance, being in 2009, after leaving Aston Martin. This was the period when I was under the hospital, eventually having an operation to sort the blockage in the Urethra. It would be around ten months before I was able to look for employment, which I found at Aston University.

When I made my decision, to retire, I gave the University plenty of notice that I was going in May 2013, when I would reach my 63rd birthday. This would give then give them time to arrange for my replacement to be appointed. At the end of May 2013, I left the University, and embarked on my life after full-time work. I was happy to consider some casual work, which I thought would give me a little pocket money for whatever activity I decided to pursue. Before, I retired, colleagues, had advised me that the University, were always looking for exam invigilators, at certain times of the year, and this may be a good area for me to look at for some casual work. When I did look into this, the exam department were happy to provide me with some work, as the fact that I had worked at the University, gave them some assurance that I would be the right sort of person to carry out the invigilator role. I did in fact carry out some invigilating prior to my leaving my full-time Purchasing job, and thought it was suitable for what I was looking for, in the way of casual work.

About six months after I had left my full-time job at the University, I was contacted by Shirley, who was the Assistant Purchasing Manager, at Aston. She told me that the Purchasing Manager, was about to leave, and they needed someone to help out, in Purchasing for about three months until they could recruit a new Purchasing Manager. She asked me if I would be interested. I said I would come in and have a chat with her. When we met, I said I did not want to work five days a week, but I would be ok with four days. It was agreed, and within a few days I was back at the University, in the Central Procurement Department, doing a similar role that I had previously been carrying out. At the end of the three months with a new Purchasing Manager, in situ, I said my final goodbye to the Purchasing Department. I was still to see the people, from that department, and Estates, when I popped in to say hello, when I was invigilating at the University.

I had played golf on and off over the years, when I could, but in all honesty cannot say that I had a aptitude for it. In fact the opposite is probably the case. For anyone who like me as toiled to achieve some sort of level of ability, on the golf course, and failed miserably, I share your frustration. I know of no other sporting activity where the more effort you put in, the worse the result. If I am asked what my handicap is, my response is usually the same, when it comes to golf, everything about the game is my handicap. The clubs, my physical ability, my brain, which fails to connect with what I am telling it to do. Slow the swing down, keep my head down, don't move my body; my brain says one thing and my body does the other.

Many years ago I was playing at Hatchford Brook Golf Course, which was close to the old Birmingham Airport. The first hole on the course has been moved now to accommodate a new clubhouse, but in those days, there was tree, about 15 yards just slightly right, in front of the old first tee. It would have been on a Sunday morning, quite busy, with many people standing around waiting to tee off. Standing on the tee with my driver poised to take my first stroke. Really hoping that it was good, so as not to look a complete idiot in front of the watching audience. A good connection but the ball flew to the right, struck the trunk of the tree, flew back over my head and landed about 15 yards behind me. With head bowed, and looking for a hole to appear and swallow me up, I collected the ball from in front of the gathered throng. I shouted, "I'll take three", and with due haste hit the ball off the tee to start my round. The problem is that I want to play golf for the exercise, the camaraderie, with my fellow golfers and friends, and even maybe one day to improve, and find some consistency in my game. Golf is one of the thing I do regularly, as part of my activities in retirement. So it looks like I am stuck with it.

I was playing golf, with Ray, my mom's younger brother, and a couple of his golfing buddies, Brian and Maurice, at West Midlands Golf Course, Balsall Common. It was around the middle of May, 2014. I remember we had just played the six hole, a par three, and weirdly had all landed in the same bunker, with our first shots. It was the seventh hole, which requires you to clear the lake, with your drive off the tee, to get onto the fairway. We had all done this, but my next two shots, on the fairway were decidedly bad, which really annoyed me. I felt a strange sensation across my chest, not a pain, but a definite irritation. I then felt faint, and needed to sit down and then lie down. I shouted to Ray, and the others that I was not feeling well. They quickly came over, and looked concerned. Maurice told me later that I was white as a sheet. One of them rang the clubhouse, and asked if someone could come over in a buggy and pick me up. As, I was travelling back to the clubhouse, I was feeling better. When we got to the clubhouse, the guy who picked me up told me to sit down, and he got me a cup of coffee. After a few minutes, Ray and the other guys appeared, to see how I was. They had decided not to continue their round. I had driven to the Golf Club, but thought it was better if I did not drive home. I rang my wife on my mobile, and asked her to come and collect me. Although, not a pain as such, I still had this irritation across my chest. It was about midday on a Friday afternoon. When Gill arrived, we made our way towards home. I decided to call into our surgery, in the hope that I could get checked out by a doctor. The receptionist said I could get an appointment, but it would be with a locum, around six o'clock. I declined the offer. She said that if I had chest pains I should dial 999. This I was not going to do. I got back in the car, and Gill asked what I wanted to do. I felt it needed to be checked out so I asked her to take me to our local hospital at Warwick. Within five minutes, of arriving at Warwick Hospital, I was talking to a triage nurse, who asked another nurse to carry out an ECG, without delay. Shortly afterwards I saw a junior doctor, who took some blood from me. I then had to wait a while, lying on a trolley in one of the cubicles. I was visited by a more senior doctor who did not seem to worried, and the results of the ECG had not caused them any concern. A little bit later he returned, and said that the first blood results had come back, and although my white blood cell count was a little high, which could mean there was some infection, generally they looked ok. He said that they were still awaiting for the result of the other blood test, which would show if there had been any problem with my heart. About, a half hour later he appeared with the results of this blood test, and advised me that it showed that I had had a heart attack, although mild. The one thing health wise was that I always thought that my heart was sound, and this was a real surprise for me. Even the doctor seemed a little surprised. It seems that when you have a heart attack, an enzyme is released into your blood. This does not always appear straight away and sometimes doctors will repeat the test, six hours after the first test. The doctor said he would admit me to the hospital, and further investigations would be carried out. Only a week before this happening, my wife and I had visited her cousin Brian, in Walsgrave Hospital, in Coventry. Brian had had a cardiac arrest whilst playing badminton, and was lucky that there were staff in the Sports Centre, who were able to resuscitate him. After tests, they found that one of this arteries was blocked, and they had inserted a couple of stents to relieve the problem. I also had an Aunty Joan, who a couple of weeks previously had suffered a heart attack. Again she had stents fitted to assist the blood flow in her arteries. They had given me some literature in the hospital, about heart attacks and their treatment. The week after

I was admitted to Hospital, I was taken over to Walsgave (University Hospital) Hospital for an angioplasty test. I was told that the test consisted of injecting a dye into your arteries, which showed what was happening to the flow around your heart. I was also advised that should the angioplasty show that one of the arteries was blocked, or narrowed, they would be able to insert a stent, at the time of doing the test. However, if they found that multiply arteries were affected, it would mean that a bypass operation would be required. I felt that with my recent experience of relatives, having what seemed to be far more serious heart problems, than myself, if I did require any treatment it would be a stent, or maybe two. When I did have the angioplasty, not a lot was said. It took about ten, fifteen minutes, and at the end the doctor informed me that all my arteries were narrowed, and I would require a bypass operation.

As I was wheeled back to the Day Ward, at Walsgrave, the nurse pushing me, asked if it was the result I expected. I responded, it was not. She said that bypass surgery was common, and they would be able to sort my heart problem out. Whilst I was returning to Warwick Hospital, the paramedic accompanying me, was also encouraging, saying that Walsgrave Hospital, had a very good reputation for heart surgery, and I could not have a better place for this operation. Back in the ward at Warwick, I was visited by one of the Doctors. He had the results from Walsgarve, and advised me that he wanted me to stay in Hospital, one so they could keep an eye on me, and two that it would speed up the time that I would get my bypass operation, which he thought would be around two weeks hence.

I was sharing a room with another guy, named David, in the Coronary Care Ward. We got on well, and sometimes our wives would go off and have a coffee and a chat, in the Hospital Café. This I think helped them. A trouble shared etc. There were certain rules that applied to visiting, in the Coronary Care Ward, which did not apply to the rest of the hospital. The thinking was that heart patients need rest, the visiting times were therefore limited, with a couple of hours in between when our lights would be switched off, and we would be encouraged to have a nap. Two visitors to a bed was also strictly observed in the Coronary Care Ward. David had been in hospital longer than myself. He had picked up a virus that had damaged one his heart valves. He was receiving treatment for the virus, and this needed to be sorted before he could have an operation to replace the heart valve. He had his own business and would work on his laptop every day. However, he was limited, by his wife, Janette, as to how much time he could work, and he knew he would be in trouble if he overran.

At times, I am ashamed to say, David and I would abuse the visiting system. If David had four visitors, and I had none, the chairs would be arranged so it looked like two were for David and two were for myself. This would sometimes be queried by the ward staff, and one or two of them would suspect foul play, but generally we got away with it. It was about ten days after the angioplasty, that I was told, that my bypass operation was scheduled for the following Tuesday. I was taken to Walgrave the day before, on the Monday. My surgeon, a smart, very pleasant Asian gentlemen, came and had quick chat with me. He said that he intended to carry out a quadruple heart bypass, as all my arteries were affected.

On the day of the operation, 10 June 2014, I was taken to the operating theatre, for the Anaesthetist to his job. I do not remember waking up as such, just to series of things, which I believe a cross between dreams and what was happening in the intensive care ward. My wife and daughter-in-law, Louise, came to see me after the operation. I have no recollection of this at all, but they tell me I was smiling, and kept trying to pull out some of the tubes, that were protruding from my chest. For this type of surgery, the hospital operate, what they call a step down system. Basically, after their operation, a patients will be in intensive care, then to a ward where they will be receiving, virtually, one to one attention of a nurse, then to a ward with a normal staff ratio, and finally to a general or side ward, before they go home. This can be over a period as short as five days, if everything goes well. I did have some problems after my operation, and my time in the one to one ward was three or four days. The fact that over the years, I have checked my own blood pressure and pulse, with a devise at home probably did not help. I found myself continuously looking at the monitor, I was connected to. I could tell, also there was some concern from the medical staff as well. I had an irregular heartbeat. My blood pressure, and pulse, were much higher than should be. When the nursing staff, looked at your monitor, went over and filled a syringe, and left it at the end of your bed, you knew, they were ready to take whatever action was necessary. The nursing staff were brilliant. Each and every one of them showed absolute dedication to their patients, were genuinely caring, and were a credit to their profession. I could have not received better treatment anywhere. Walsgrave Hospital, or the University Hospital of Coventry and Warwickshire, as it is correctly named, provided me with the best possible treatment, and whenever the NHS is criticized, all I can say is that the treatment I received was second to none.

The day after my operation, I saw my surgeon had a brief chat with me, when he said that my operation had gone well. He returned to see me three or four days later. He then told me that he had carried out a triple heat bypass. My arteries were soft, and although he was able to complete the first three, when it came to doing the fourth one, it was difficult. He had tried for some time, to attach the forth one, but it was dangerous to extend the operation for too long, and he had decided that with three done, it was safer to finish the operation at that point. He said that he had since spoken to the Cardiologist, and it should be possible to insert a stent, if this was necessary in the future. He said that he thought my arteries had softened as a result of the long term use of steroids. This I discussed with a transplant consultants a few months later, at my next outpatient's visit. Her opinion was that it was not the steroids, but the general effect of my kidney illness, over the years. Whatever the cause of this problem with my arteries, I cannot complain. The drugs have given me well over thirty years of pretty much a normal life, even if they have adversely affected my arteries, and virtually every drug has a side effect of some sort. In my case I don't even have to consider whether it's was worth it. I did wonder whether, the condition of my arteries had been a factor, as to why jogging had been a struggle, in recent years (old age and injuries permitting), and whether once the surgery had settled down, I may be able to do a bit of regular running again.

I was actually in hospital for eight days, before I returned home, with a booklet telling me what I could and could not do for the next few weeks. The main things, were related to the fact that my chest had been opened up, and the re-jointing of my ribs, needed to heal. Heavy lifting was prohibited, as was mowing the lawn, golf, and ironing, for the next twelve weeks. Gill pointed out, I never did any ironing anyway. There was a requirement to gradually walk a little bit more every day, starting with a couple of laps around the house. The problem with was that as part of the operation, a vein is removed from your leg, to use as the bypass, around the heart. This was obviously something that my left leg was not keen on, as it became swollen to about three times the width of my right leg. For the first two or three weeks, my wife, and the district nurse who came to dress my leg initially, encouraged me to walk normally, which is not easy when one leg is three times the size of the other. They said I was dragging my left leg, instead of let it take its turn to lead, with the other leg, and if I continued I would always walk like that. My response was something like, "well you try walking properly, with one leg three times the size of the other," and sometimes a few other words would be included in this statement. Luckily, after about a month, my leg returned to its normal size, and walking became much easier. After about six weeks I was walking to our local Newsagent, about a mile and half away, every morning, and then included some extra distance as the weeks progressed. After about four months I did a few holes at my local golf course, with my friend Paul. This was the nine hole golf course surrounded by Warwick Race Course. With my usually accuracy one of my golf balls, landed just short of the five furlong point, on the Race Course. Not a bad distance, I thought for a man just recovering from heart surgery. Paul told me afterwards that he was so concerned about me having another heart attack, on my first venture back on the golf course that he had researched what to do, in that situation. He was ready at any time to thump my chest, should I collapse showing the signs of cardiac arrest. Luckily, this did not happen, and I was soon regularly playing as badly as ever on the golf course.

About three months after the surgery, I had a appointment to see my Surgeon, at Walsgrave. He enquired how I was feeling, and asked how things had gone since the operation. I was able to give him a positive report. He said that I did have an irregular heartbeat at first, but this had now corrected itself, and all was looking good. I asked if I would need to see him again, and he said no, but the Cardiologist may wish to keep an eye on me. About a month later I did see the Cardiologist. He was happy with the way thing were going, and said he could see me every few months , if I wished, or I could just go back to my GP, if I had any concerns, and they could refer me back to him. I said I was happy to leave it at that. As it stands I am feeling really well, playing golf !, and doing some Exam Invigilating work, as and when required by Aston University, and my local school in Warwick.

The Epilogue

One of the reasons I wrote this book, is because a young doctor, who I saw when I went for one of my six monthly check ups suggested I document my experience, which he thought would be useful for young doctors like himself. I could understand his thinking as most patients he sees would be on a different drugs regime, to myself and other long term transplant patients. In the early 1980's a new 'wonder drug' cyclosporine, came onto the scene. As far as I am aware all new patients from that point were on that drug. There were however initial problems with cyclosporine in that it turned out to be toxic to the kidney. Various work was done and although it was continued to be used it was given in very specific doses etc. When I am speak to people who are recent transplant recipients, they tell me they are on many more drugs than myself, and have to take them at specific times. I wondered whether the medical professional have carried out any research on how patients taking cyclosporine, and the supplementary drugs, compare long term, with old patients like myself, taking the original anti-rejection drugs.

When I think about what has happened to me during my life, the word that keeps coming back is how 'lucky' I have been, in every respect. Lucky in terms of timing and support; if my kidney problems had started five years earlier, I may not have received dialysis, with the resulting consequences, also in terms of the start of the Transplant Games, in the same year I had my transplant, lucky with the start of mass marathons, in the early 80's in this country; if I had not had the supporting family that I had, I may not have been included on the dialysis programme, and the support of all my family with my activities throughout the years. Last but not least, lucky to be a match, when a family, at a time of great loss for them, were so generous to think of someone else and give the gift of life.